From the Bench and Beyond

Behind the Scenes in Sports---
One Guy's Perspective!

Mostly humorous, occasionally serious, possibly inspiring and sometimes almost unbelievable true stories of what you don't see or hear when it comes to being a fan of baseball, football, tennis, running and other sports.

The bench, the courts, on the roads, the dorm or maybe the practice field. That's where the real action often takes place!

By

Lyle M. Gibson

Dedication

To my wife Janice who has "put up with" my obsessions in sports by supporting me through the good times, as-well-as the not-so-good times. Don't forget, you have your own little behind the scenes sports story that helped to put us on the road to forty-three years of marriage. That day, long ago when you secretly signed us up for the Oak Street Junior High School "Mixed Doubles Table Tennis Tournament" and then accused me of doing it was a bit low and underhanded. But, from a positive standpoint, it did help me get to know and "like" you a little more at the time. By-the-way, if you had taken some time to practice your backhand, we wouldn't have finished second. Regardless, thank you for a wonderful life. I love you.

Also to my three sons, Jason, Justin and Jonn. To my daughter in laws, Kacee and Lizzie. To my grandchildren, Conner, Carsen, Jenna and Ryan and to my in-laws, Don and Vivian Kellar.

To my father, Arlo who I miss. He passed away in 1990.

And a special dedication to my mother, Dorothy who I know will read this book at least three times.

Thank you to Craig T. Neises, a terrific photographer, who supplied photos for this book, including the cover and the inside shots.

Thanks to Chuck Brockett, General Manager of the Burlington Bees, Class A affiliate of the Los Angeles Angels Baseball Club, for allowing us to shoot our photos at "Community Field"---home field of the Bees and the same field our high school team called "home" in the "old days".

Special thanks to my good friend and long-time running buddy, Russ Fry. An incredibly talented runner, writer, film-maker and speaker whose expertise allowed me to put my memories and thoughts that follow into a book.

Preface

I think most would agree that the United States is a "sports crazy" nation. A high percentage of citizens enjoy watching their favorite athlete or sports team compete on a regular basis.

Spectators come in many categories. At one end of the spectrum you have the casual fan, as-well-as the "built-in" fan of a youth or high school athlete. The opposite extreme has the fanatical face-painted, wig wearing, sign carrying, near psycho cases that live and die by their favorite college or professional sports teams.

Fans at all levels watch sports from metal bleachers, lawn chairs, expensive stadium seats and from comfy couches and recliners at home. Three-year olds to professional stars, there's such a wide variety of ages and skill levels to root for.

A fan's perspective of most of the athletic contests they watch is often one-dimensional. Basically, what they see is what they get. They're aware of little more than what they observe on a field or a court at any given time.

But, there's a remarkable side of sports that the average fan never gets to experience. This includes an infinite number of behind the scenes antics, rituals, pranks and unexpected occurrences involving the players and coaches. With athletes' personalities ranging from the quiet and studious, to the boisterous and even borderline insane, the stories are unlimited. Some are hilarious, some a little more serious, some maybe not so nice and others close to unbelievable. Certain stories passed on through the years can even take on a legendary status to some.

Athletes ranging from three-year-old tee-ballers and soccer players all the way to ninety-year old slow-pitch softball players have stories to tell that may have little or nothing to do with actual on-the-field competition.

I have been very fortunate to have played and coached sports with so many great people. There are so many stories that it would take a lifetime to put together a full collection of my behind-the-scenes stories.

This book is divided into three sections. *Section I* is a grouping of stories that begin when I was an athlete in junior high school and ends upon graduation from college. *Section II* are true tales that I experienced as an adult participant in several sports such as tennis, running, racquetball and adult baseball. *Section III* are stories from my adult involvement as a coach of kids in a variety of sports and in a number of age groups.

Some of the following "adventures" will be the first time my mother has heard the "real story". In this case, it is honestly, I admit, a cowardly confession years after the fact. Sorry Mom. I think I'm too old now to be grounded at this point in my life, but maybe some of the guilt I've held inside for so many years will be dissolved.

It is my desire that you find these stories fun, entertaining or maybe even educational. I also hope it gives you a somewhat different perspective of sports in general. The stories are true, names have been withheld in most instances to protect the guilty. Please, just call me Sam.

Table of Contents

SECTION I----------------STORIES FROM A YOUTH PARTICIPANT   Page

Chapter 1------------------Halls of Shame   11

Chapter 2------------------The Broken Play   17

Chapter 3------------------Signs of the Times   23

Chapter 4------------------The Junior Lettermen   31

Chapter 5------------------Up in Arms   37

Chapter 6------------------Sounds From the Mound   43

Chapter 7------------------College Dorm Form   49

Chapter 8------------------Dumb Jocks Defined   55

Chapter 9------------------D. J. Associate Members   63

SECTION II------------STORIES FROM AN ADULT PARTICIPANT

Chapter 10---------------An Unusual Court Case   69

Chapter 11---------------Tennis Bum Chums   73

Chapter 12---------------Long Distance Looniness   81

Chapter 13---------------Running Back to the Future   89

Table of Contents Continued

Chapter 14----------------Running Math---Obsession + Compulsion Equals 95

Chapter 15----------------Runners: Tall True Tree Tales 103

Chapter 16----------------Runners---Personality Question Marks 113

Chapter 17----------------Shine or Rain---It's only Pain 123

Chapter 18----------------Senior Moments---Athletic Style 129

SECTION III----------STORIES FROM A COACH

Chapter 19----------------Tee Ball by the Numbers 135

Chapter 20----------------The Traveling Team Dilemma 139

Chapter 21----------------How to Lead by Example---Not! 143

Chapter 22----------------More Adults We Can Do Without 147

Table of Contents Continued

Chapter 23----------------Coaches' Capers   153

Chapter 24----------------Kids Do the

                      Weirdest Things!   159

Chapter 25---------------The Never Concluding

                      Conclusion   167

About the Author------   171

Section 1

(Stories from a Youth Participant)

CHAPTER 1   *Halls of Shame*

It was the late sixties. At that time, Oak Street Junior High School in Burlington, Iowa consisted of grades seven through nine. I was in the eighth grade.

Our eighth grade basketball coach also happened to be one of the school's physical education instructors. Believe me, this man had his work cut out for him each and every day. Whether he was teaching in the gymnasium or putting extra time in after the school day trying to mold our "Bobcats" basketball team into something it never was--- a good team.

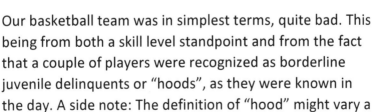

Our basketball team was in simplest terms, quite bad. This being from both a skill level standpoint and from the fact that a couple of players were recognized as borderline juvenile delinquents or "hoods", as they were known in the day. A side note: The definition of "hood" might vary a touch depending on who you spoke to. Often times, at least from my point of view, a "hood" generally seemed to be students who lit up a cigarette at the conclusion of many things. End of class---light a cigarette, end of the school day---time for a quick drag. After practice---light it up! A "hood" also seemed to be a somewhat part time student, skipping classes consistently, but somehow just scraping by and being promoted to the next grade. "Hoods" quite often seemed to have a fight scheduled with someone, but rarely ever fought. Anyway, "win" was not a word that was thrown around much with our basketball team for two main reasons. First, certain players might have had some difficulty even trying to spell the word and second, since our team never won there was little reason to use the word. I was a starter, one of our better players I would guess, but that fact truly meant little other than I was pretty much assured of plenty of playing time. To say we were a team that lacked pure talent would be a definite understatement.

What we lacked in raw talent we made up for in obnoxiousness and a lack of discipline. It had to be a frustrating experience all the way around for Coach "?" (Name withheld to protect the identity of the poor guy and his family)

Many members of our team probably preferred riding the bench as opposed to playing in actual game situations. It was typically more fun horsing around on the bench than going through the usual agony that took place on the court. This is somewhat understandable as a high percentage of our games consisted of running up and down the court and tossing the ball inbounds way too many times after a basket by the opposing team.

One day our "P.E." class was semi-lined up against the wall waiting for Coach "?" to arrive to begin class. We were in our standard waiting mode which consisted of a great deal of yelling, including the usual name calling and occasional four-letter words. Pushing, shoving and punches to the arm were routine. Honestly, I always considered myself one of the more "in control" kids. I didn't use profanity and refrained from mini-boxing and wrestling encounters. To be honest, punches to the arm and headlocks just plain hurt!

Coach "?" eventually arrived and began his explanation of the activities that would be taking place in the class that day.

Truthfully, I don't recall what the coach said we were going to do, but whatever it was failed to impress me. It sounded like a waste of fifty good minutes which could have been used more wisely. I wasn't thinking (How many eighth graders actually have mastered this skill, anyway?). In my frustration, I blurted out but one word: "Whoopee!"

"Whoopee"---that's all I said! That one word was way more than enough. Coach "?" must have been experiencing what was probably a typical bad day. Whatever the reason, he certainly didn't care for my two syllable evaluation. "What did you say", he shot back at me.

I said, "Whoopee!" This time with much less enthusiasm. Coach "?" turned several lovely shades of red that I hadn't seen before on a male and immediately began heading in my direction. I assumed he was about to grab my arm and either drag me to a corner of the gym or out in the hallway to sit for the remainder of the class period. Worse yet, he might march me into the principal's office which could lead to eternal detention or worse yet, expulsion. Whatever the consequences, I remember thinking this was not going to set well with my parents once they found out.

Rather than "take it like a man", for some inexplicable reason, (keep in mind, thinking and eighth-graders are mutually exclusive) I started running from the coach. Yes, running! Much to my surprise, the coach started running after me! I headed out the side door of the gym, took a sharp right and began jogging down the hallway. I glanced over my shoulder and I couldn't believe my eyes. Coach "?" was still coming after me! "Uh oh", I thought; "I'm a dead man!" I broke into a sprint, turned right at the corner, then a sudden left and immediately headed up the steps to the buildings' second floor. When I reached the top of the steps, I could hear the coach's heavy footsteps approaching.

He obviously wasn't concerned about sneaking up on me, but there was no doubt he certainly meant business. I circled the upper floor with a determined, persistent, crazed educator/coach in hot pursuit. Heading back down to the first floor, I quickly turned left, shot through a door that led to the stage of the school's auditorium. I raced across the stage, still hearing the echo of footsteps in the distance. I threw open a door at the back corner of the stage and headed into what was the girl's locker room.

Fortunately (or unfortunately depending, on how you look at it) the room was unoccupied at the time. I quickly opened the next door in sequence and entered the boy's locker room. From there, having completed a full loop of the school, I headed back into the gym. Back to the place where this whole fiasco had begun. Laughter filled the room as I ran across the gym floor for a second time and scampered through the same door I had exited less than five minutes earlier.

This time, rather than turning right, I chose to go left and head down a stairway to the lower level of the building. It appeared Coach "?" had finally aborted his seek and destroy mission. God forbid, he was laying on the floor in cardiac arrest. I decided to take no chances and waited until I was certain the pitter-patter of big feet had ceased. I hid for the rest of the class time, as well as the following class period in an unoccupied, darkened, music room.

When I finally came out of hiding, I peeked into the gym to make certain the coast was clear. It appeared to be, so I proceeded to slip into the locker room and change back into my street clothes. I went to my final class of the day; the whole while waiting for Coach "?" and/or the principal to break through the door and whisk me away in handcuffs or maybe a strait jacket. It never happened. The school day came to an end and I somehow had been able to remain in one piece. Amazing!

Uh oh, it suddenly hit me that I had basketball practice at 3:30 p.m. That would surely be where my demise would begin. I hesitantly changed into my practice gear and began to mentally prepare myself for the certain ambush. I went out on the court hyper-ventilating and began shooting around with my teammates, waiting for Coach "?" to appear. I was convinced he would be asking me to turn in my uniform within minutes. Finally Coach "?" made his entrance and I thought to myself, "Here it comes!" Instead, he merely asked the team to form two lines and begin a traditional two-line team lay-up drill. Still not a word. Practice came and went. I was still physically intact. The rest of the week came and went. I was untouched, but it was taking its toll on my frazzled nervous system. The month came and went. The school year came and went. Unbelievable! I was free.

I never suffered the deserving consequences of my actions. To this day, I have no idea how I "got out of that one". Absolute blind luck? Could have been. Totally blind lack of justice. That's a definite. Mostly however, I think it was an overloaded brain by Coach "?", who just plain forgot or more likely, wanted to forget the whole ordeal, thus diminishing the messy paperwork and certain meetings that would surely come with the situation. Whatever the case, I was one lucky boy.

CHAPTER 2   *The Broken Play*

About ten months after my race through the hallways, I was a ninth-grader at Oak Street Junior High School. A little taller, just slightly heavier, same coach, but now a different sport. This was the "big time". Junior high school "varsity" football.

Coach "?" was a multi-sport coach, who pretty much had to "do it all", when it came to attempting to mold boys into upstanding young men via sports. As with last year's eighth grade basketball team, he definitely could have used a much larger mold. The football team consisted of pretty much the same "athletes" who had participated on last year's basketball team, only now with the addition of fifteen to twenty "student/athletes". As a whole, most of these guys had even less natural athletic ability than those who had played basketball. Many however, just plain liked hitting people. While not necessarily in prime condition, these were typically some of the physically bigger kids in the school.

As you undoubtedly know, being capable of knocking someone's lights out and being larger than the average teen-ager certainly doesn't have a direct correlation with being an outstanding football player. Our team could have easily confirmed this in a controlled scientific study.

With the first game of the football season scheduled in September, junior and senior high schools in Iowa start formal practices in the scorching heat and high humidity of August. It's a short time frame of only a few weeks from the beginning of a team's first practice session to the team's first game of the season. So, in order to be up to full speed by the season opener, schools generally run practice two times per day, right up to game day. These "two-a-days" didn't seem to be overly beneficial for the Oak Street Bobcat football squad. Practicing twice a day seemed to have a straight "dose relationship". In other words, practicing once in the morning and then a second time each afternoon, may have made us twice as inept. It's a well-known saying in sports that a team will "play like it practices". So, it only made sense that practicing the way we did with our limited capabilities, did nothing to improve our squad once the first game of the season rolled around.

The initial game day eventually arrived. There were three junior high schools in the city of Burlington, Iowa and we were scheduled to play the best of the three schools. Our game was to be played on what turned out to be a gorgeous, warm mid-September Saturday morning at Bracewell Stadium, home field of our local high school team, the Burlington Grayhounds. Bracewell Stadium has to be one of the most beautiful settings anywhere in the country for high school football. It's located in the middle of the city and is set well below street level in a wooded ravine. The stadium has the distinction of being the first high school football stadium in the United States to host a night game under artificial lighting. It was an exciting place to play. The knowledge that we were such a poor team gave way to thoughts of doing great things this day on the turf of this storied stadium.

Unfortunately, great things were not in the cards for our team. It wasn't long before it became obvious Coach "?" and his Fighting Bobcats were over-matched.

As is often the case for football programs at the junior high school level, a number of players had more than one responsibility. I was no exception. On offense I started at wide receiver and was a back-up running back. On defense, I played safety. I was also one of our team's kick-off and punt returners. To top it off, I was the team's punter.

The first quarter squelched our pre-game dreams of greatness, as the opposing team scored two quick touchdowns. My only claim to fame was I caught one pass for a first down, knocked down a long pass while playing safety, and got off two or three punts that at least headed down field in the right direction. It was long ago, but I believe the first quarter ended with our motley squad down by a score of fourteen to zero. While I certainly wasn't a star, I seemed to hold my own without embarrassment.

Early in the second quarter, the opposing team had quickly moved the football steadily downfield and were positioned somewhere near the fifty yard line. Then came "The Play". Their quarterback handed off to their team's star running back. This kid was big, strong and fast. He had up to this point, pretty much manhandled our defensive line. This run was no different, with the exception that on this play he not only broke through our line, but he also side-stepped past our line-backers and cornerbacks. He was heading in my general direction. "Help me, God. Please help me!" I thought to myself. I knew as our team's safety, I was our last resort to stop the human Clydesdale galloping down the field. I raced at an angle towards him, took a mighty leap and in mid-air was able to wrap both arms around him, just below his knees. Down he went. It had to look like a pretty good play from the stands, but down on the field was a different story all-together. The big running back, who probably outweighed me by thirty or forty pounds came tumbling to the ground. No touchdown this time for the human wrecking ball.

There was definitely some give and take on this play. As he landed, my right arm happened to be directly under his body. My arm was somehow pointing straight up with my elbow on the ground and my fingers in the air. As he landed on my arm, I literally heard a loud "snap!" "This is not going to be good," I surmised. It was an understatement.

An incredible pain shot through my right arm as I slowly stood up. When I looked at my arm, it was literally dangling from just above the wrist. I slowly jogged toward the sideline, absolutely positive my arm was broken in a big way.

I sat there in agony for what seemed like an eternity when all of a sudden Coach "?" shouted: "Gibson, get in there and punt! Looks like we'll need to tape that arm. Go punt and then we'll do that." "Coach", I said, "I can't punt, my arm is broke!" "Gibson!" the coach shot back, "I can't believe it. You milk toast! Oh, just forget it!" "Milk toast"? Sticks and stones and football players may break my bones, but words can never hurt me. I really didn't care what the coach thought I was, because my arm was now in one more piece than it was supposed to be. No more football today.

I remember walking home after the game carrying all my football gear with my left arm and excruciating pain coming from my limp right arm. Nearly a mile of pure agony. I arrived to an empty house, as both my parents were at work. When my mother finally arrived, we immediately went to the hospital where an x-ray confirmed a clean break of my right wrist. The fracture ended my football career, forever.

I went to school that following Monday with a new cast and a sling holding the cast and my arm at a right angle. When I saw Coach "?", all he said was: "Wow, I guess you did break your arm. That's really too bad. Looks like your season is over." Good call, Coach Obvious.

Yes, I was a "milk toast" who had eight long weeks of healing time in front of me.

CHAPTER 3   *Signs of the Times*

The "head" baseball coach. This is a man or woman, regardless of the level of play, who strives to develop a team into a well-oiled machine. To be successful, this person must possess a multitude of talents. He or she certainly must be knowledgeable about the rules of the game. This individual needs to be familiar with not only the basic fundamentals of the game, but to be a consistent winner, must have a grasp of some of the finer points. Organizational skills is most definitely a key component. A successful head coach must be a gambler of sorts, and not be afraid of rolling the dice in crucial game situations.

A top-flight coach must know how to blend a number of unique personalities into a single unit that has a special personality all its' own. To make it all come together, the head coach needs to be the ultimate communicator, able to instruct in a way that an entire team understands. An outstanding coach is able to encourage and motivate players in a positive way all season long.

Great communication makes a huge difference. The difference between a talented team that consistently wins a large number of close games, as opposed to a team that often comes out on the short end of the close ones.

Following are two separate stories of miscommunication. The first story comes from a youth baseball team I played for and the second from my college baseball playing days.

The first story I can honestly say was no ones' fault but my own. The second story? You can make the call.

I was thirteen years old, playing Pony League baseball. Pony League was the next step up the age-group ladder after Little League baseball for boys living in Burlington, Iowa back in the 1960's.

Our team was being coached by two young men, both of whom had just completed their freshman year at the University of Iowa. In reality, these guys weren't much older than the players they were coaching.

Our team, in comparison to the other teams in our small six-team league, was actually a pretty solid squad. In fact, by season's end, we were champions of the league.

Looking back, I truly think our young head coach had an exceptionally strong knowledge of the game for his age. Combined with an incredibly dry sense of humor, it proved to be an enjoyable summer of baseball. The players loved him and chose to listen carefully to his "words of wisdom" during practice. This proved to pay off, as we practiced hard, laughed hard and then practiced hard some more. Our coach, regardless of his youthfulness, had gained our respect. All said, we were generally well-prepared to play when game day rolled around.

One positive aspect of our leader's coaching method was the simplicity he kept in the game. A prime example would be the signals he gave to our batters and our base runners when coaching third base. He believed, as I do today, that signals should be easy to understand at all times for a couple of reasons. First, in order to avoid confusion, simple is a no-brainer as compared to complex. Too much to remember jumbles a young boy's mind and takes the fun out of what is supposed to be an enjoyable game. There's already so much to be concerned with. Secondly, no matter what the situation calls for, such as a stolen base or a hit and run, if the player or players execute the called play properly, there's nothing the opposition can do to stop it. Even if the competition knows it's coming, there's not a darn thing they can do about it. Perfect offensive execution will win out time after time.

Prior to one of our mid-season games, our coach decided to change the signals we'd been using. He explained although the signals were new, they once again would be quite simple. It was time to change the signals, as he assumed the other teams might be picking up on our original ones after having played approximately ten games. For reasons I don't recall, during the instructional session, a teammate and I chose to have a conversation among ourselves rather than pay close attention to the explanation of the new signs.

Several innings into the game, I came to the plate with runners on first and second base and no one out. The coach began flashing his simple new signs in my direction. Since I had chosen not to pay attention during the pre-game instruction, I had no clue as to what the signs meant. I stared at the coach dumbfounded. Apparently he thought I had just missed the signal the first time around and went through the signs a second time. Once again I again stood there like a "deer in the headlights". This time I just shrugged my shoulders and shook my head. The poor coach dropped his head, put his hands on his knees and then shook his head in disbelief. He held that position for what seemed like forever. He suddenly shot straight up, stared at me and pointed to a spot in the grass; a tiny area about half way between home plate and third base and approximately five to six feet inside the foul line in fair territory. "Gibson!" he yelled loudly. "Lay the ball down! Bunt it---right there!" He wanted me to lay down a sacrifice bunt in order to advance each of our two baserunners one base. Laughter was everywhere. The crowd, both dugouts, me and finally, even the coach joined in.

The next pitch, I proceeded to put a bunt down pretty close to the target our coach had just specified. Both runners advanced. A pretty good sacrifice bunt if I do say so myself. It would have been a lot simpler and a lot less embarrassing, if I had just learned the new signs in the first place. Poor communication on my part. I was fortunate the outcome ended on a good note.

My second communication (or should I say lack of communication) episode took place while playing baseball during my sophomore year in college.

Our head coach was a young (thirtyish) man who was relatively new to coaching at the college level. He was a former Triple A catcher in the Baltimore Orioles organization, having been given his release only several years earlier.

Our team had an abundance of talent. Players had been recruited from such far-away places as California, New

York, New Jersey, Missouri, Minnesota and Pennsylvania. Other than our top catcher, I was the only starter from Iowa. Most of the players were on full-ride scholarships, including myself. I tell you this to make a point.

An abundance of natural ability does not alone correlate into a fantastic team. In fact, this team, as good as it should have been, started off the spring quite poorly on a southern trip to Tennessee, Mississippi and Louisiana. We came back with really nice tans and a zero and eight record. We didn't win a single game! We also lost our home-opening double header, giving us not one win and double figures in losses in the young season.

To help deal with our frustration we came up with a team "rap" before the word "rap" was part of the American jargon. We added a "verse" to it after each loss. It went something like this: "We're zero and one, today wasn't fun." "Zero and two, we're not yet through." "Zero and three, what's the key?" "Zero and four, good chance we'll do it some more." "Zero and five, are we even alive?" "Zero and six, we're taking our licks." "Zero and seven, this sure isn't heaven." "Zero and eight, not feeling too great." "Zero and nine, this isn't so fine." "Zero and ten, good God, we did it again."

Then it happened. A minor miracle? A victory! "One and ten, let's win again and again!" While we were a team loaded with talent, we were obviously not showing much of our true capabilities. What could be the reason for this? I have at least one theory.

Our coach, unlike my young Pony League coach who worked in a simplistic way, and discovered it to be successful, approached the game with a one-hundred and eighty degree outlook on communicating signals to his players. A very complicated system to say the very least.

We figured this poor guy must have spent time in the CIA, as his system of signals needed special agents to break the code. Ordinary college baseball players certainly couldn't do it. He had developed the most elaborate, confusing, possibly ridiculous set of coaching signals since the invention of baseball.

There were pre "double indicator" signs to set the actual signals that had true meaning into motion. He had swipes across the chest; one, two, three and sometimes even four. They all meant something different. There was numerous hand claps, pulling of the ears, tapping of the nose and tugging on the bill of his cap. He left very few body parts untouched! There were slaps of both thighs and the stomach. He even had a confusing set of "wipe off" signs in order to cancel out the twenty to thirty previous signs. This was done in order to start the entire signaling process over from scratch.

If you happened to be the hitter, you might have time to read a short novel while the coach completed his signals. It was unbelievable!

I honestly can say of the twenty or so players on the team, not one of us knew the signs: Ever! I honestly question whether the coach was ever totally sure of what he had directed his hitter and/or baserunner(s) to do. The signals were that confusing.

I was the lead-off hitter for the squad. I would literally steal second or third base, sacrifice bunt or hit and run, when I felt the situation called for it. Other players chose to do nothing after missing a sign and suffered the wrath of the coach once the inning ended.

Now you would think most coaches at the constant requests of his players would eventually give up and make things easier all the way around. It didn't happen. He was stubborn and stuck by his guns. He was apparently convinced that this was the best way  to communicate (?) to his team. His theory seemed to be that if no one in the ball park, except for our team, knew what was going to take place, the odds were in our favor. It made perfect sense. The problem, of course, was our team didn't have a clue either. This went on for the entire season.

My salvation during the season, was never once getting thrown out stealing a base and never once failing to get a sacrifice bunt down to advance a base runner or runners. Combined with hitting well over .300, I was fortunate enough to avoid the big doghouse many of my fellow teammates often found themselves in.

It can safely be said that it was a long season for many of us. The constant strain of not having any idea of what we were supposed to do on the field took its toll psychologically on the team. Regardless of the lack of coach/player communication, talent won out slightly. We actually finished with a winning record, a game or two over .500. No telling how well this team could have been if they knew what they were supposed to do in key situations, and didn't have to run scared when they didn't. Good communication and we "could have been a contender!"

CHAPTER 4 *The Junior Lettermen*

As a high school junior, I was a reluctant member of the Burlington, Iowa High School cross country team. I had no choice. I wanted to play varsity basketball. To do this, it was a rule of the school's athletic department that any potential candidate who wished to try out for the basketball team was required to participate on the fall cross country team. The theory behind this, was that all candidates would arrive at the first day of basketball tryouts in prime condition. They then, wouldn't have to depend on tryouts, to work themselves in to shape.

 Apparently it wasn't well thought out that running on the cross country team would give us limited time to practice shooting, dribbling, rebounding, passing or playing defense.

The majority of the basketball hopefuls had little desire to run long distances day after day for two solid months. I happened to fall into the category, the "forced to do something I really, really disliked" category.

Funny, I really wasn't too bad at the whole running thing. I just didn't care for it. A fellow teammate and good friend of mine had the same negative feelings about running as I did. Together we chose not to find out what our true abilities were as distance runners. There was no formal planning by my buddy and myself to slack off for an entire season. But through some form of human osmosis, we understood that we would do the least amount of work possible to earn our varsity letter. I now look back at this time, not having a great deal of pride in the way I chose to handle this part of my athletic career.

The school's head basketball coach also served as the head coach of the cross country team. A former small college All-American basketball player standing in the neighborhood of six foot-six or six-foot seven inches, now indicates to me that there's a good possibility that he had very little actual cross country experience as a runner. As a coach, I believe he gave it his best effort and probably studied a great deal about the sport from books and/or articles from the running experts of the day. Looking back, I think there's a very good chance that our coach knew a good deal more about the sport than we ever gave him credit for.

He had many positive personal characteristics. He had a great sense of humor and had a wonderful ability to treat every participant with the same level of respect regardless of the athlete's talent.

In a high school cross country meet, typically all, or at least a majority of the team, runs the race at the same time. The standard high school cross country course is five kilometers, just over three miles. Scoring is figured by assigning a score to only the top five runners on the team. Each of these five runners are given the same point value as their actual finishing place in the race. For example, if one of your team's runners finished first, he or she would be awarded one point. The second place finisher receives two points, the third three points and so it goes. You add the points of your team's top five finishers together to get your total team score. The team who scores the least amount of points is declared the winner.

While we failed to work to be the best we could be, my buddy and I were both still proficient enough to consistently finish in or close to the top five in the majority of our meets.

Our team did most of our practice running on the same course (the local public golf course) that doubled as our home course for competition.

My friend and I spent most practices producing the least amount of sweat that we possibly could. This included running until we were out of sight of the coach and then hiding behind a group of trees. When the rest of the team, who had run the full course, came back by our hiding place, we once again joined them. We ran less than half the distance the rest of our teammates had. We figured what the coach didn't know, certainly wouldn't hurt him.

The school had an early season tradition. For reasons still unknown to me, we held one or two "meets" on a running track. All of the members of teams from three different schools (called a "triangular meet") would toe the starting line. Everyone would then proceed to run a mile which was four laps of the track. Scoring consisted of standard cross country scoring, with only the top five runners from each team receiving points to be tallied to determine the winning team.

Before one of these cross country "track" meets, my friend and I cooked up what we thought to be a humorous little prank. It consisted of us starting to run what looked like a warm-up lap, with each of us taking off at the same time, but in opposite directions on the track. When we met face-to-face on the far side of the track, we "faked" a major collision, with both of us falling to the ground in what appeared to be writhing pain and agony. We yelled and moaned as our teammates came running in our direction, with the coach following closely behind. An Academy Award nomination should have been in order for our performance. "You guys all right? What happened?" The coach was truly concerned. We could only hold it in for a matter of seconds. We burst into laughter simultaneously. The coach did not see the comic genius of the prank like the vast majority of the high school audience present. He didn't even crack a smile. He just shook his head in disgust and walked away. The meet went on. I ran well enough to finish fourth or fifth for the team that day. Not bad. The coach never once mentioned the incident the rest of the evening.

The season trudged on and much to our pleasure, finally came to an end. The final wrap-up to the season was the much dreaded post season awards ceremony. This one, as most were at that time, was held in the school gymnasium in front of the entire student body and faculty. After the coach finished his inspiring speech he began handing out "varsity" letters.

My friend and I waited for our names to be called. We waited and waited. Our names never came during the varsity portion of the program. Instead, ours were the final two names called during the junior varsity awards presentation. One after the other, with red faces, we sheepishly walked to the podium to receive our "junior varsity" letter. Yes sir, the coach had waited until the end of the season, the very last minute, for a little payback and to prove a point. Point being, a lack of effort and screwing off will not be tolerated. We were thoroughly embarrassed and humiliated. Of course there's little doubt we deserved it. Lesson definitely learned!

CHAPTER 5   *Up in Arms*

I've played many different sports over my lifetime, but baseball is where I was able to find success to some degree at every level in which I participated. From Little League to high school to college and even into upper middle age at the Fifty and Sixty and Over National Baseball Championships. Whenever a person asks me what my favorite sport is, there's never any hesitation--- "Baseball!" So many fond memories center on the sport.

Some of my proudest moments in baseball came at Burlington (Iowa) High School. Burlington High School was an Iowa prep baseball powerhouse during the sixties and seventies. Being an All-State player and leading our team in hitting for such outstanding teams are true highlights.

 Following closely behind, is the day I first saw my name posted on the glass of a trophy case at the school, announcing that I had actually made the team. I was a freshman. As a freshman in Burlington, Iowa, nothing could be sweeter than being a Grayhound baseball player. It was a great program year-after-year. Burlington High School had the distinction of winning the first ever state baseball championship in Iowa.

The school also held another "first" when it came to high school baseball. It was the first high school in the United States to have "bat girls"! Several years before, the Iowa State University baseball team was the first collegiate team to field a bat girl squad. While I've long since realized how sexist the whole thing was, I have to admit at the time I thought it to be incredibly cool.

Our Bat Girl Squad consisted of seven or eight junior and senior girls who were assigned various game duties. This included the traditional tasks that young bat boys had been doing for decades, plus additional assignments. Included were such things as retrieving bats around home plate after a hitter dropped his bat and began his sprint for first base or beyond. They also took baseballs to the home plate umpire when his supply had dwindled. Another job was chasing down foul balls both inside and outside of the stadium. This array of duties was more than enough to keep the squad consistently active throughout the traditional doubleheaders our team was accustomed to.

To become a bat girl was no easy task. Gaining entrance into the Harvard School of Law might have been somewhat less demanding. Our head baseball coach, Dick Wagner, whose idea it was to initiate this lovely new addition to school's baseball program, didn't make it easy for any girl who aspired to be a team member. A prospective bat girl, first and foremost, had to be a top-notch student. Athletic ability was a non-factor. These were not cheerleaders. These girls were to be respected, hard-working members of a top quality high school baseball program. They were going to be true representatives of our school.

Coach Wagner had the girls who were interested in becoming a member of the squad, fill out an essay form. Here, they were asked to highlight their reasons for wanting to be a bat girl. I give up, why would anyone want to be a bat girl? After this, Coach Wagner and the team captain sat down and reviewed the "applications" and then scheduled face-to-face "interviews" to make the final selections.

Honestly, it was a very high quality group of girls. Smart, attractive and ready to go to work.

The season opener eventually arrived. It was scheduled, as usual, to be a double-header. Our "home field" in those days happened to be "Community Field", which was also the home field of the professional Class A, Burlington Bees. The Bees at that time were an affiliate of the Major League's Oakland "A's". It was a beautiful stadium with a wooden grandstand that was painted green and had gorgeous trellis-work hanging from the edge of the roof. It had a capacity approaching three-thousand. In those days our high baseball team often out-drew the professional team due to the outstanding marketing and public relations work of our coach, Dick Wagner. This night would easily prove that statement to be true as the crowd was extremely large. These were the days when the students had little else to do and fully supported their team. So did parents, brothers, sisters, grandparents and many residents of the community. With the night's addition of the highly publicized debut of the nation's first ever high school bat girls' squad, it obviously made the crowd swell even more.

Prior to the game all the girls were introduced by the public address announcer and soon the first game of the evening began, as did the work of the bat girls.

As "boys will be boys", there were a few cracks made in the dugout by some of the team members. Nothing mean or outrageous. Just little comments like: "Hey look, Bill, she has a better arm than you do!" "Boy, Jerry, if you could run as fast as her, you'd never get thrown out stealing second!" "Hey Steve, I've seen you in shorts, she sure has you beat!" "Maybe the girls will distract their pitcher enough that he'll walk a ton of us." But in reality, I think the players were somewhat proud to be a little part of history. If nothing else, we wouldn't have to chase the foul balls like we had in the past.

The first inning or two went well that night. Our team started out playing good baseball and took a comfortable early lead after scoring several runs. The bat girls quietly and with the exception of their short purple shorts, went about doing their jobs pretty much unnoticed. Foul balls were retrieved at once, bats were picked up quickly and the umpires were supplied with fresh baseballs when the need arose. They did a great job and looked great doing it. It appeared the squad was going to be a very nice addition.

In an effort to make things as fair as possible and maybe just to relieve potential boredom, the girls apparently had pre-planned to rotate duties. This took place somewhere around the middle of the first game. Those who were earlier chasing foul balls would now be picking up bats at home plate and returning them to the bat rack or hustling baseballs out to the home plate umpire.

It must have been around the bottom of the fourth inning when our lead-off batter reached first base after connecting for a base hit.

The girl whose new duty was to retrieve the discarded bat near home plate was apparently extra eager in the debut of her new assignment. Standing near the dugout, she broke towards home plate like an Olympic sprinter out of the blocks. She was "pumped"! She raced towards the bat with such a blast of raw energy that she found herself unable to slow down. As luck would have it, she stepped squarely on a round bat. Square and round didn't mix well. Her foot rolled the bat enough that she lost all sense of control. Both her legs and both her arms flew straight up in the air and she landed hard on the back of her head and upper back. She lay there stunned for a few seconds as the crowd gasped. The players in the dugout rolled their eyes, turned and looked the other way as their faces turned various shades of red. Sure, we felt bad for her, but at the same time, I think we collectively took it as semi-blow to our team; in a juvenile sort of way. Although the girl's lack of grace was hers' and hers' alone; I believe some of the players on the team felt it was a reflection on them. Don't forget, these were high school boys, many lacking a great deal of maturity.

Fortunately, the poor girl was fine. No major injuries, except to her ego. The game continued and the incident was pretty much forgotten. But, not completely. Forty-five years later, as you can see, I obviously still remember it. In fact, I remember it well. I would have given her a "9" on form and overall grace. The Russian judge? I'm guessing a "6" at best.

CHAPTER 6   *Sounds From the Mound*

Baseball is a great game! It's the "The National Past Time". Very little has changed with the basic rules of the game in approximately one-hundred and fifty years. Through it all, it still remains one of, if not the most difficult, sport to master.

Its' pasture-like setting can give you a sense of peace and tranquility when watching it. On the field it can be filled with remarkable athletic abilities and an infinite amount of strategy. The game can have beauty and grace that can rival a classic ballet at times, or a hard-nosed battle of two longtime enemies at other times. The game also takes the intelligence and patience of world class chess-masters when two top-notch coaches try to outthink each other inning after inning.

From the high school level on up, the game is a unique combination of science, strategy and incredible skills with a touch of blind luck thrown in to make it even more interesting. All these factors blend into the making of an exciting, complex game.

We routinely see players or both players and coaches gathering on the pitchers' mound or other areas of the field to discuss various matters. Maybe a player or coach spots something mechanically incorrect in the pitcher's delivery. It could be how to pitch to a particular hitter or maybe how to set up defensively based on the situation.

There's often a great deal of serious, strategic conversation that takes place in just a single baseball game.

But there's also the "secret" discussions that take place on the little dirt hill that literally have nothing to do with the game of baseball. Coaches deserve a golden brick road to heaven for some of the things that takes place on the mound. Some examples:

My junior year of high school, I was doing a fair share of catching due to the loss of our top two "backstops". I won't go into the circumstances that caused our team to suddenly be "catcher-less", but I was reluctantly called into duty early in the season.

We happened to be playing a smaller school that we outright overmatched. Our pitcher was doing a fine job on the mound. This player happened to be a true perfectionist, however, and was not overly satisfied with his performance. We were up sixteen to zero and he had given up only one or two hits and struck out the majority of batters he had faced. This was through the first three innings. I had already made one trip to the mound to try and calm him down after he had given up a base hit. Can you imagine what he would have been like had we been down sixteen to zero?

In the fourth inning the first batter eked out an infield hit. Heaven forbid! "Mr. Happy" then walked the next batter, putting runners on first and second bases with no one out. It appeared a

stroke might be in order for our flustered hurler.

As he looked in towards me for his sign, I decided this poor guy needed a little something to loosen him up. I planned to call for his best pitch, a fastball. The traditional fastball signal in baseball is for the catcher to simply put his index finger straight down, hiding it from the opposing team by placing it well back between his legs. I did everything in the traditional manner, with the exception of using my index finger for the sign. I decided to use my middle finger instead. As you probably are aware of, an extended middle finger has another "unofficial" meaning and it isn't "fastball".

At first, our grumpy flame-thrower stared and then stared some more. He then stepped off the pitcher's rubber and just shook his head. Disgust? Confusion? Sheer anger? I'm not quite sure. Maybe a little of all three. He regained his composure, stepped back on the rubber and looked in for his sign once again. I decided to not let him off the hook and flashed him the same dual-purpose finger signal one more time.

This time, something must have hit home and he again stepped off the rubber. He was laughing uncontrollably. I called "time out" and jogged out to the mound. At the same time, Coach Wagner was making his way to the mound to see what the commotion was all about.

The coach asked what was going on. I explained that our pitcher seemed a little "tight" and I was just trying to relax him a bit. I was told by Coach Wagner that "He's loose enough now. Let's just keep this thing moving."

Final score: twenty-one to one. Thank goodness it wasn't a close game. Psychological therapy for our pitcher would have cost the school a mint!

There were a couple of other mound visits in high school that involved words rather than "gestures".

One of these consisted of our pitcher signaling me out to the mound to inform me that his friend was working at McDonalds that night and had told him to be sure and stop in after the game. If we made certain to go to his cash register, he would hook us up with some "free" hamburgers. After our victories that night, we made a quick trip to "Mickey D's", where I ordered a Coke, fries and a hamburger. I ended up enjoying a Coke, fries and three hamburgers. We had hit the jackpot! Of course, in 1970 a hamburger was only twenty-five cents. Wow, we had walked away with fifty cents worth of free food!

A team mound meeting during another high school game was a serious strategy session to determine who was going to, and more importantly, who would be driving to, a post-game party at the home of one of our bat girls. It ended up being a crucial meeting that saved us a good minute or two after the game. It's all about time management when you're in high school.

The last memories of mound round tables were from my college days. There were the usual time outs that were used to point out a great looking girl in the bleachers; but there's one meeting of our infielders, catcher and pitcher that really stands out. This meeting took place prior to the start of an inning after our first baseman rallied the guys to the center of the infield. I happened to be good friends with the first baseman. Prior to the team meeting on the mound, he had just ask me if I would want to join him for an weekend rock concert that featured some up and coming young star. He had one extra ticket to the show. I reluctantly said "no" as I had planned to spend Saturday night with my future wife. I don't remember which player finally accepted his offer, but one of them eventually did. So while Janice and I spent Saturday night going to a movie and then for a pizza; my two teammates were rocking' to the "The Crocodile Rock" by some new singer/pianist by the name of Elton John.

I know I made the right decision.

CHAPTER 7 *College Dorm Form*

The college years can be some of the best, most exciting years of a person's life. This is especially true if you're an athlete who's been fortunate enough to be having a good baseball career.

I would have to say this was my case, with the exception of the extraordinary amount of injuries I suffered my final two years. The injuries put me in the role of designated hitter. But playing four years of college baseball was still extremely memorable. In more ways than one.

I had one unbelievable season where I hit an even .500. The ball seemed like it was as big as a beach ball and in slow motion as the pitchers threw their best at me all season long. I also committed a combined total of only one error while playing second base my freshman and sophomore seasons. Serving the team in a designated hitter role my junior and senior years, was not what I would have preferred, but at least I was still playing baseball.

As a freshman from a small city in southeastern Iowa heading to college in Mankato, Minnesota (now Minnesota State University), I look back now and realize how confident and mature I was as an athlete, but how naïve I was at life in general.

I lived on the tenth floor, the very top floor of the dorm my freshman year. The tenth floor was reserved for the school's athletes. My best guess is the administration put the athletes as high as possible in order to get them as far away from humanity as they could. Another possibility might be that the school's top brass put the jocks on the top floor in an effort to be as close as possible to God, hoping that the athletes might experience some sort of divine intervention and maybe show the poor lost souls "the way". I lean towards my initial theory, because if it was theory number two, it was a total failure.

My roommate happened to be a very good varsity swimmer, one of the best on our college team. I think he had much more potential than he ever displayed, due to his undisciplined lifestyle. He took his new-found freedom away from his parents to the upper limits. I often found myself staying in my first baseman buddy's room at night. Why? Because my part time swimmer friend and full time "ladies' man" of a roommate often times entertained an overnight "guest". More than once, I walked in on "lover boy" attempting to add to his already well-established reputation.

In the room next to my roommate and myself, lived the two starting defensive tackles on varsity football team. One stood six-foot four inches and weighed in at a not-so-sleek two-hundred and eighty pounds. The other checked in at six-foot five inches and made the scales cry out in pain, weighing in at two-hundred and eighty-five pounds. Hilarious guys both of them, but both the type you definitely want on your side if any type of brawl would break out.

Our "floor" formed a basketball team to enter the college's intramural basketball league. This meant our team was made up of athletes of all varieties, with the exception of varsity basketball players. I was our "outside" threat and our two football tackles made for a formidable duo inside. A football running back and a hockey player rounded out our starting five.

In the next to last game of our league schedule, the center for the opposing team, who had actually played high school basketball, was playing a very aggressive defense against our six-foot five tackle who was moonlighting as a center. He kept leaning in and putting a body on our big boy. The kid was somewhere close to six-foot seven or six-foot eight, but was probably not more than one-hundred and eighty pounds. He was a human toothpick.

Having someone playing real defense against him, finally got to be too much for our mammoth inside guy. In a split second, our "center" pivoted swiftly around and with a powerful right hook smashed the beanpole squarely in the middle of the jaw. The poor guy was actually airborne as he landed on his back and slid a good five or six feet on the hardwood. The blow could likely be heard back at our dorm. The punch literally shattered the poor kid's jaw. I had never seen one human hit another human so hard. This signaled the end of two players' basketball seasons.

One with a broken jaw and one who was banished from the league.

A second related dorm episode occurred in that same glorious freshman year. In Minnesota, the sport of hockey ranks right up there with football, baseball and basketball. Two doors down from our dorm room lived two hockey players, one who happened to be the starting goalie on the varsity team.

I may be stereotyping, but hockey players appear to be a different breed of animal all their own. They seem to lean heavily towards the wacky side. From my observations, the goalie apparently is quite often the "head wacko"! This was unquestionably the case on our college team anyway.

One night as my roommate and I were both sound asleep in our beds (my roomie had no visitors this particular evening), we were both awakened by a major commotion in the hallway. It was approaching three o'clock a.m.! We shot up and rushed to the door to see what the ordeal was all about. When I opened the door, my roommate and I peeked around the corner where we saw the two hockey players in the hallway. They were racing in our direction with the goalie in hot pursuit of his team mate. The goalie was carrying his hockey stick, wearing his over-sized shin pads, donning his goalie mask and wearing absolutely nothing else! My roommate and I came to the conclusion that this particular goalie had been hit in the head by a few hockey pucks too many!

Our baseball team had swept a long double-header at Winona State University earlier that day. By the time we finished in the early evening, stopped for a relaxed victory celebration dinner and made the lengthy ride home in the team vans and unloaded, I finally reached my dorm room sometime shortly after midnight. I was ready to get some sleep, but I was filthy dirty and sweaty from a day on the diamond. I thought to myself how good a shower would feel and help me sleep more comfortably. So, a shower it was.

I took off my baseball uniform, wrapped a towel around my waist and headed to the men's "community shower" located in the center section of our dorm's tenth floor. A quick reminder, this floor was dedicated to the male athletes of the school. I heard a shower running as I approached the shower room door. I didn't think twice as I opened the door, just as I had well over a hundred times before. In fact, as I entered, I expected to see one of my teammates who had the same idea as me. I removed my towel as I stepped foot on the tiled floor. As I turned the corner, much to my surprise, there was a lovely young woman taking a shower by herself.

Don't forget, I was pretty much a prude from southeastern Iowa. I quickly put my towel back on (really) as she looked in my direction. I apologized to her for the interruption, even though it was "my shower", and began heading towards the door. As I walked out of the room, she called back to me: "Hey, that's o.k., you don't have to go." But I told her to "have a good shower." "Have a good shower?" I guess "prude" was an understatement!

College life can be filled with temptations and as I've stated previously, baseball players don't necessarily have to be that smart. In this situation there's not a single doubt in my mind that I made the correct decision that particular night. But, I chose not to tell any of my team mates my decision on this one.

CHAPTER 8 *Dumb Jocks Defined*

The term "dumb jock" is thrown around a good deal. It's a stereotype often given to athletes in general. I would guess the term has a somewhat similar connotation, regardless of who you talk to. My guess is the derogatory label was most likely initiated by a jealous non-athlete. A simple definition? A human being with gifted athletic abilities who possesses the brain and reasoning power of a chimpanzee.

The term is somewhat unfair as there are many, many intelligent athletes who have gone on to great things outside of the sports world. Some have gone unto distinguished careers in medicine, science, music and politics. Okay, maybe politics is a poor example. In fact, the many former athletes who went into politics may be where "dumb jock" got its start.

I will admit, there are a number of talented athletes who only enter college to play high quality athletics and could care less about receiving a top level education. There are also the occasional athletes who do unusual things away from the playing arena who do their part to keep the "dumb jock" label alive and well.

Here are several stories from my college baseball playing days that pertain to athletes and their antics that don't necessarily put them on the waiting list to Brain Surgery "U".

Our team was in Jackson, Tennessee. We were standing at a lowly zero and six record. Following our sixth defeat, eight members of the team (I was not one of the eight) decided a "night out on the town" might be just the ticket to boost the team's spirits and get us on the winning track.

After sunset, five starting position players, one starting pitcher and two subs snuck out of the motel's side door and crowded into one our team's two extended vans. They then proceeded to head downtown. I chose not be involved in this escapade, as I saw trouble written all over it. The episode took place soon after all involved were certain our head coach had retired to his room for the night.

My roommate, who happened to be one of the participants in the "great escape" woke me when he swayed into our room somewhere around five o'clock in the morning. He felt obligated to wake me up and fill me in on the details of the team renegades' adventures.

Their first stop was at a downtown bar, where they met several co-eds from one of the area colleges. The girls were heading to a party and whether invited or not, my run-away teammates found themselves at the same party. Although not a drinker, I do know that good looking college co-eds, cheap wine and beer, together with college baseball players, are not an ideal combination. This especially holds true for a team trying to get things heading in a positive direction.

Eight hours of alcohol, women and whatever came with it, provided a state of physical and mental exhaustion, not to mention significant headaches of a very high magnitude.

Later that day our team lost another double-header, leaving our record standing at a miserable zero and eight. Our team was not over-matched in talent that day. In fact, I would say we were definitely the better team on paper. We were, however, greatly over-matched in team discipline.

There's no doubt that the college baseball team I played for my sophomore year had a disastrous start to the season. To a group of athletes who are used to winning, an extremely poor start can have a demoralizing effect that can quickly spread through a team. It can make players who love the game all of a sudden despise practice and even more so, really not even enjoy competition.

There's a scene in the motion picture "Bull Durham" where the minor league baseball team, the *Durham Bulls* had a major losing streak of their own taking place. Several players, led by Kevin Costner's character "Crash Davis", are talking about how much they wish the next days' game would be rained out so could have a day off. "Crash" says he can personally take care of their wish. Without hesitation, the players sneak into the stadium where the team is to play the next day. "Crash" proceeds to locate the main water valve that controls the field's sprinkler system. He turns the water on, leaving it to flood the field well into the next morning, making the field unplayable. "Rainout" taken care of without any rain.

A situation very similar to this took place my sophomore season in college. I can safely say I was innocent on this one and had no part in it. Well, no part other than I refused to give the names of the guilty participants when the head coach was asking for perpetrator names.

After a zero and ten start to our season, several seniors decided the team needed a break. So, in the late evening, the day before a scheduled double-header, three of our senior "leaders" headed to our baseball field located on the edge of town.

The field didn't have an elaborate sprinkler system. Instead it had two water faucets located near the first base dugout and two more located near the third base dugout. Long hoses were attached to each, giving a total of four hoses to take care of the fields' water needs.

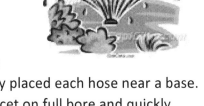

The players connected the four hoses and strategically placed each hose near a base. They then turned each faucet on full bore and quickly exited the scene of the crime.

When the groundskeepers showed up the next morning to prepare the field for the early afternoon double-header, the entire infield was under water. Mission accomplished. No games that day!

The story didn't end there, however. Our coach scheduled a "surprise practice" for later that day. Although he never found out who the culprits were, he knew it was members of the team, of course.

Practice that day was deemed "the practice from hell" by the team. It lasted a good three hours and was not even close to being a traditional practice. There was very little hitting, fielding or throwing of baseballs. The majority of practice consisted of wind sprints, agility drills and distance running. It was exhausting and the point was clearly made.

We also manned rakes, buckets, squeegees and sand as we removed a lake full of water from the diamond to prepare it for the re-scheduled double-header the next day. It was a day of hard physical exercise followed by hard physical labor.

It must have worked, as the next day we actually won our first game of the season! Discipline can have its' rewards.

Major League baseball players have been notorious throughout the years for partaking in the disgusting habit of chewing tobacco. Chewing has, of course, been proven to possess negative health issues and has since been banned from professional baseball.

In my college days (the seventies), it was quite common for a good number of college players to indulge with a "little pinch between their cheek and gums".

I got the impression that to most players, this wasn't necessarily a pleasurable habit, but more of a status symbol, a sign of masculinity. It was an indulgence that may have made many players feel, from a psychological standpoint, one step closer to being a major leaguer.

I was our team's starting second baseman my sophomore season in college. Our back-up second baseman/shortstop, was a very good player. He was highly recruited out of the state of Pennsylvania. I know he was disappointed that he lacked much playing time, but we became good friends just the same. He was one of my biggest supporters and a great teammate.

One late afternoon as the sun was about to set and the shadows were long, we were finishing up a practice. All of our infielders were taking a few final ground balls before we called it a day. We were tired, maybe a little lackadaisical and it was getting tough to see.

Our back-up second baseman and I were alternating taking grounders. He was taking what was to have been one of his last balls of the day, when the ball he was preparing to field came whistling at him hugging the ground. Without warning, the ball hit a rock or clump of dirt and at the last split second shot straight up striking him squarely in his Adam's apple.

Now being hit in the throat with a baseball is painful enough, but this poor guy was also a chewer of tobacco. Once the ball collided with his Adam's apple, the wad of tobacco found its' way directly down his throat. What followed was not pretty. My player/friend went down to his knees immediately. Next, his normal rosy cheeks began changing colors, finally settling on a pale green shade. After a back and forth series of gagging and vomiting, he eventually ended up flat on his back for a long while in an obviously uncomfortable "wait-it-out" period. All-in-all, it was a pretty disgusting display.

I will say, our formally macho, tobacco chewing infielder became a bubble gum chewer for the remainder of the season.

CHAPTER 9   *D. J. Associate Members*

I was smart enough (or at least lucky enough) to avoid a good share of incidents which contributed to enhancing the "dumb jock" label. But, I was personally involved in several events that gave me more of what I would call an "associate dumb jock" status, rather than full blown membership into the club.

One incident happened while our college baseball team was taking the school's annual spring swing through several southern states. We were in Hattiesburg, Mississippi at the time. It was only the second day of our trip. We had played a double-header the day before, so we only had a total of two games under our belt for the young season.

I had a good start to the season in the previous days' games. As the teams' lead-off hitter, I had gone three for seven with a single, two doubles, two RBI's and two stolen bases.

I was pumped, confident and anticipating another good day. We had our best left handed pitcher going for us. He had pinpoint control, a sharp-breaking curveball and a very good fastball. In my mind, this was going to be the beginning of good things to come for our squad.

As I often had for several years, I moseyed down to the bullpen as our hurler was warming up prior to the start of the game. I liked to stand next to the plate and eyeball a few pitches to help get my timing down and to focus on seeing the spin of the ball. Whether it helped or not, it was a standard routine and helped me prepare for the game, at least from a psychological standpoint.

It was a hot, humid day and a light mist was falling. Our pitcher was good and loose and throwing hard. He stated that he "felt great" and was "ready to go".

About that time, it happened. Whether the light rain was the culprit, making the ball slippery or the pitch just got away from him, he launched a fast ball that was heading directly at me! I had no place to go and didn't even know which way to turn to avoid disaster. The ball hit me, hard! It struck me squarely in the left kneecap. Ouch! The kneecap, of course, has virtually no padding. The pain was about as intense as any I had ever experienced. I instantly went down.

I was helped to the dugout by two of my teammates who acted as human crutches, with one player on either side of me. Sitting in the dugout while waiting for our squad to complete two baseball games was agonizing. I did not have a good feeling about the potential outcome of the situation as I sat there waiting for the games to end. It hurt even worse, knowing I was not only out of the line-up for the day's games, but surely would miss a number of games in the future.

After the games ended, the coach took me to a local hospital where tests concluded I had fractured my kneecap.

This confirmed there would be no possibility of playing during the remainder of our southern trip. I spent the next week at our games, in the warm sunshine, sitting shirtless and wearing gym shorts in the stands. It was not all leisure, however, as I became the team's official scorekeeper and also charted our pitchers during the games.

All was not lost however. I came back to Iowa a week later with a .429 batting average for the two games I did get to play and I did get a great tan!

This entire season was not a good one from a health standpoint. I had been battered and bruised all year long, beginning with the kneecap. I had also pulled a hamstring, pulled a groin muscle and had severely twisted an ankle by mid-season.

The final straw came while playing second base near the end of the season against a college in the St. Louis area. We were winning the game at the time. I already had two doubles and several RBI's, so I was good and psyched. The opposition had one out and a runner on first base. Our team was looking for a solid ground ball that we could turn a double play on and finish out the inning.

The right handed batter swung hard and gave us exactly what we were looking for. He hit a solid ground ball right at our third baseman. Playing second base, I took off to cover the bag, expecting to catch the throw from our third baseman, and then relay the ball on to our first baseman to complete the "twin-killing".

As I circled into the second base bag, I received a perfect, chest-high throw from our third baseman. As I had done literally hundreds of times before, I caught the ball and took a full step towards the third base side of the infield to avoid colliding with the oncoming baserunner.

Remember the term "dumb jock"? I can't verify this, but the big boy bearing down on me quite possibly fit the stereotype. He proceeded to go a good three feet or more out of the baseline and with his arms crossed. He flew into me head first at full bore hitting me in my lower legs. My feet went straight up and I came down, landing on the back of my head with such force that it knocked me completely unconscious.

The next thing I remember was "coming to" in the grass adjacent to our dugout located along the first base line. Our coach was waving a broken ammonia capsule under my nose. I recall having a headache that just wouldn't stop!

I was diagnosed with a concussion at a nearby medical clinic shortly after the incident. It seemed a fitting end to a season filled with injury after injury. In fact, at the team's year-end awards banquet, I jokingly received the teams' "Red Cross Award" for "injuries above and beyond the call of duty".

Oh, and what became of the "unethical" brute of a runner in that fateful game? Well, he was definitely out in more ways than one. First the umpire ejected him for intentionally going out of the baseline to plow me over. To top it off, the ump also found the ball our third baseman had thrown me, was still in my glove! Through it all---I had held on to the ball!

The next year our college team was taking our early season spring trip to Panama City Beach, Florida.

It was a most enjoyable experience, as I had never been to Florida before. The Gulf of Mexico, and white sandy beaches, along with eighty-degree temperatures had to be a small taste of what heaven was like.

We were to play Brooklyn College on a perfect, warm, sunny day. Our team arrived early at the field to take a lengthy session of batting practice. One-by-one my teammates came to the plate, laid down a practice bunt or two and then proceeded to swing away, in search of making perfect contact with the baseball.

I came up somewhere in the middle of the group, took my bunting practice and then started to swing aggressively. I was seeing the ball well and was spraying a fair share of line drives to all fields. Our coach, who throwing batting practice, placed a fastball on the inner half of the plate about waist high. I swung and hit it squarely, right on the "sweet spot". The ball jumped off my thirty-three and one half inch wooden Adirondack "Jackie Robinson Model" bat, with that beautiful sound a baseball makes when striking a bat near perfection.

The ball sailed well over the canvas covered left-center field fence about three-hundred and fifty feet from home plate. It was the first homerun anyone had hit in practice up to that point.

One of our outfielders volunteered to retrieve the ball. Off he went and quickly disappeared behind the outfield fence. Seconds later, we all noticed our ball-retrieving teammate literally sprinting back towards the diamond. He was screaming words he really shouldn't have been in a public place. We noticed he was also empty handed. No baseball.

"What's wrong?" "What's the matter?" players were asking. Breathlessly, but enthusiastically, he shouted out: "There's a #@/*ing alligator out there!" The ball had landed in a swampy area just beyond the fence approximately five feet from the "biggest alligator in the world!" And as he stated: "There's no way I was going to pick up that ball, I ain't stupid, ya know!?"

He was definitely a better baseball player than an English student.

Section 2

(Stories from an Adult Participant)

CHAPTER 10   *An Unusual Court Case*

As stated previously, baseball was and still is my favorite sport. Unfortunately, unless you're lucky enough to play at the professional level or at least live in an area that's large enough to support an adult baseball league, a baseball career can come to a screeching halt after college.

I did get to play a little "semi-pro" baseball the summer after graduation, but the writing was on the wall. Injuries suffered in college limited me to a reduced role as a designated hitter my final two years.

It was time to find something new to pursue. So that I did. It came in the form of coaching tennis and making myself into a good enough player to hit the Midwest tournament circuit. The majority of the tournaments I participated in were held in Iowa and Illinois.

There are several, what I would call, "interesting" behind the scene tennis stories. I'll get to one of them a little later, in a future chapter. Before I talk tennis, I want to discuss a personal story that involved another sport that used a different type of racquet and ball.

While playing tennis, I found myself also playing a fair amount of racquetball. I played the game to help in developing my overall quickness and increase eye/hand coordination for tennis. I have to admit tennis and racquetball are two distinct sports with totally different ways of stroking the ball. I chose to play racquetball using the same basic strokes I used in tennis, however. This worked well for me, at least against the players I was competing with.

I was playing the game enough that I decided to enter the "City Racquetball Tournament". It was held annually at the local YMCA. As I recall, there were three divisions in singles. The "A" division was for the best players in the area, the local "elite". Few players in the area fell into this category. I hadn't been playing that long, so I didn't feel I was ready for the top level. I was pretty sure that natural ability alone put me above the "C" division. The "B" division. That had to be where I belonged. So, that's the division I entered.

The sixteen-man draw was to be held over a weekend, with the first round and quarter-finals to be held on Saturday. The semi-finals and final were to be completed the following day on Sunday afternoon.

My Saturday matches proved to be relatively easy. I breezed through the first round and the quarter-finals without any problems. A match consisted of winning two out of three games. To win a single game, a player had to be the first to score fifteen points and be ahead by a minimum of two points. I won four games and didn't lose any that first day against my two opponents. I ended up winning all the games by a wide margin.

The next day, my semi-final match proved somewhat tougher, but I still managed to win the first two games. The first game was close with me winning by a small margin. The second game was tough, but not nearly as close. Regardless, I was in the finals that was to be played later in the afternoon. I went home to rest and invited my family to come with me to watch the championship match.

We showed up for the finals a little early, so I decided to go out on the court and warm up a little, while I waited for my opponent to arrive. There was a fairly sizable crowd on hand to watch the three division championships that would be held simultaneously on three of the four courts at the YMCA racquetball complex.

About ten minutes later, the door to the court swung open and in staggered (literally) my opponent. This guy was "plastered" in a major way. While I had spent time since my initial match resting and psyching myself up for the big match, my competition was getting himself in a relaxed state by "hitting the bottle", maybe several bottles.

I said something to the tournament director and he spoke to the highly "sloshed" finalist. Much to my surprise, the director came back and explained to me that he was going to allow this poor devil to play! I couldn't believe it!

I reluctantly agreed and tried to exchange greetings with my opponent. He stuttered and spit out a few hard to understand words, in English, I think. I heard a few giggles and sneers coming from the gallery. I just wanted to get this ordeal over with. My opponent won the toss and elected to serve first. I literally had to walk up and show him where the service box lines were that he was to stand in to begin the match.

The match took all of fifteen minutes to complete. Final score: fifteen to zero, fifteen to zero. This poor sucker didn't score a single point in the entire match! Honestly, it was more than embarrassing! I accepted my first place trophy and never once felt good about it. I have never played in another racquetball tournament since.

Moral of the story? Don't drink and try to drive---a racquetball into a wall.

CHAPTER 11   *Tennis Bum Chums*

I was just beginning to understand the fundamentals, the strategies and even the science involved behind the game of tennis. Studying the best players locally and the best in the world on television helped considerably. Probably more beneficial than anything, was my constant reading about the game, how to play it, and its' long history. The books were authored by many of the past and present greats of the sport. To go with all this study and self-education, I put in hours and hours on the courts, practicing what I'd learned and observed. I got to the point where I felt ready to venture out on the local and regional tournament circuit to test myself against some of the best players around.

I made many good friends through tennis in a short period of time. There was always someone calling me to play or me calling someone for the same purpose.

A good tennis buddy and myself decided to spend a couple of days playing in both the singles and doubles divisions of the well-know and highly regarded *Miller High Life Open* tournament, held annually in Ottumwa, Iowa. This particular tournament, partly due to its' central location and excellent facilities, was frequented year-after-year by the finest players from the states of Iowa, Illinois, Missouri, Minnesota and Nebraska. The event always started on a Friday night and ran through the weekend, with the championship matches being held on Sunday afternoon at the Ottumwa Country Club tennis courts.

The level of talent was very high. So high, in fact, that my playing partner and I only took one extra change of tennis clothes to the tournament. We both assumed that we would never survive doubles and even more so, singles into the final day of the competition.

Friday night we each played one singles match and played a doubles match together. While my friend lost his opening singles match, we won our doubles match and I scraped by in my singles match. I won in two hard-fought straight sets. That guaranteed me at least one more singles match and another doubles match the next morning. To me the tournament was already a success, having won two opening round matches. It was off to a cheap motel to get some rest and get back on the courts on Saturday.

Saturday began early for me. With still thirty-two men left in the singles portion of the tournament, I was scheduled to play my second round match at eight o'clock a.m. About half asleep when I arrived, I must have been overly relaxed or too tired to know or care. I was experiencing no sense of nervousness, just swinging the racquet free and easy. My shots were hitting the mark regularly and everything just seemed to come together. I definitely played better than the previous night. I was feeling good. The win put me in the round of sixteen. It was a great confidence builder. This was originally as far as I expected to advance in the tournament with any luck. Amazing how well a person is capable of playing with their eyes half closed!!

Shortly after the conclusion of my singles win, my doubles partner and I headed to a set of courts in another section of town to begin our second round doubles match. An hour and a half later, we had done it again---we won. Although it took us three sets to do so, we had advanced into the afternoons' quarter-finals.

Before we were to play doubles again, I was scheduled to play yet another singles match. As is typical in the better tournaments, as the rounds progress, so does the level of the talent increase. I was to play a very good player from Minnesota. In my last match I had played as good as or better than ever before, and this made the match seem evenly balanced. Several weeks before this, I probably would have felt totally over-matched. Not this day, however. I felt like I belonged on the court with my opponent.

I played strong throughout, and never wavered. Although he took the first set six games to four, I still had a good feeling about the final outcome. I reciprocated and won the second set six games to four, setting up the deciding third set to determine the winner. I broke serve at four games all and then served out the match to win a long hard-fought match. Suddenly, I was now in the quarter-finals of the Miller High Life Open Tennis Tournament! Wow! It was truly unexpected, to say the least. The next singles match was scheduled sometime around nine o'clock that evening.

Prior to playing singles again, my partner and I had the little task of playing our quarter-final doubles match. As much as I would have loved to win the match, for my partner, it didn't happen. We fell in two quick sets, maybe partially due to my fatigue from the previous number of matches and the lack of rest the day had brought.

Thank goodness, I did have some time to relax before I set foot on the court to play my fifth match of the day and my seventh match in the past twenty-nine hours! In the back of my mind, I have to admit, I thought this next match would most likely end my tennis for the weekend.

Obviously, I advanced much farther than I could have ever imagined. Tired, but happy to be in the position I was, I played with both a physical and mental looseness I was not accustomed to, as if I had nothing to lose. I won in two relatively brief sets. I sensed an overwhelming fatigue both mentally and physically creeping into my opponent and it was working in my favor. I got a good shot of adrenaline and a second wind, and it payed off.

Honestly, I had expected to be sleeping in my own bed that night. But, I was in Sunday's semi-final match scheduled at ten o'clock in the morning.

My doubles partner once again had to share a room with me. We were relegated to the same old rundown motel that we had occupied the previous night. Of course, my friend didn't have a lot of choices, since I drove to the tournament and he was my passenger. I felt bad for him, but that's life on the tennis circuit.

We again paid for a room, both knowing we were nearly out money. On top of it all, I had no fresh tennis clothes to change into for my big match the next morning.

We dined late that night on a bag of potato chips and a bottle of Pepsi. After all the tennis I had played that day, I had no problem what-so-ever falling asleep.

The next morning, after taking a shower, I put on the same set of clothes I had worn on the first night of the tournament. The clothes were now wrinkled beyond belief. They pretty much defeated the purpose of the shower I had taken. I had forgotten to bring a razor, so I was heading into my third day with massive facial stubble.

We again munched on chips and had another bottle of Pepsi. Not exactly the "breakfast of champions". We soon headed to the country club to prepare for the match. I looked like part tennis player and part bum; certainly not the typical look that such a beautiful country club was used to or expected.

There was a fairly large crowd on hand for the semi-final match. I was to play a very good player from Des Moines, Iowa on one court, while the other semi-final match was to take place simultaneously two courts down. It had one player from Missouri and another from Illinois.

The second semi-final match finished long before mine did as the player from Illinois, a big lefty whizzed through the match in no time flat. I wasn't as fortunate. My match went three sets, as my opponent won the first set six games to two and I took the next two sets by the scores of seven games to five and six games to three. It was tough and tiring, but very exciting. I was going to be playing in the tournament championship match at two o'clock that afternoon. I couldn't believe it! I quickly called home to inform my wife and to see if she might be able to make the hour and thirty minute drive from home to see the finals.

I had a couple of hours to relax before the final was to begin. My friend and I decided to head to the tournament headquarters to get in some much needed air conditioning and hopefully find a little food and drink. With our last two meals consisting of chips and Pepsi, we were in luck! There was free popcorn and of all things (keep in mind, this was the Miller High Life Open) free beer! I'm not a drinker, but it was cold, so I had a nice big cup to cool off and quench my thirst. About the time we were to head back to the courts, I decided to have another cup of beer for the road. Possibly a mistake, I thought to myself, but free is free!

I must have been one scary sight when I showed up at the country club to take the court for the finals. I sported a scraggly beard. I was wearing smelly, sweaty, wrinkled clothes and I had a head of uncombed hair. To top it off, I probably had one too many cups of beer. But I was relaxed and ready to play!

I was thrilled to see my wife along with the wife of my doubles partner was there when we arrived. I knew I would have at least three people rooting for me.

The match began and we both were playing well. There were a number of long rallies, sharp volleys and a good number of service aces. I won the first set six games to four. The second set was nearly identical, but my opponent took it six games to four. It was two evenly matched players on this particular day.

At this tournament, due to the large number of matches, sets that were tied at six games all, were settled with a special "nine-point tie-breaker". With this set-up, the first player to reach five points would win the set. If the tie-breaker went to four points all, the next point won. There was no having to win by two points, it was true "sudden death".

Of course, the third set went to a tie-breaker. And, to make life a little more interesting, the tie-breaker naturally went to four points all. So, if my opponent won the point, he won the match. If I won the point, I would be champ. He was serving. He ripped his first serve in my direction. What would have likely been an ace to end the match, luckily caught the tape on top on the net and fell back on his side of the court. Second serve to come.

I made the decision immediately that I was going to take his second serve, slice the ball with underspin short to the middle of his court. This would take away his angles and force him to move in and have to hit up on the ball. If I pulled this off, I then planned to rush the net, where hopefully, I could put away a volley or a short overhead smash.

My strategy worked even better than I had planned. My shot landed where I had hoped. As I charged the net, he hit up on the ball, but it never reached my side of the court. Instead it hit the tape and fell back into his court. The element of surprise had done it. I was the new Miller High Life Open tennis champion!

The ride home was a really good one. I had to glance at my huge trophy on several occasions to be sure it was all for real.

Yes, it was a sweet ride home that day. The smell coming from the car on the other hand?

CHAPTER 12   *Long Distance Looniness*

Tennis brought about some great times, great competition and great memories. The game also while non-lucrative, brought with it the most enjoyable means of making a living I've ever experienced.

In the world of competitive tennis, somewhere around the age of thirty, you're near or possibly even slightly past your prime. Top flight tournament tennis is a young man's game and I was crossing over that fine line that was once my best playing days. I was coming to grips with the fact that it was time to move on.

I knew I was going to actually have to begin "working for a living". I took a position as the District Marketing Supervisor for the local utility company. While I truly enjoyed my job, I missed being in motion and I missed competing. I had a void to fill that baseball and now tennis had left in my life.

The hole was soon filled to over-flowing when I discovered a passion for distance running. For years I had avoided running like the plague. The sport seemed too lack any real meaning, it appeared very boring and was exceptionally time consuming.

This whole thought process changed on my thirtieth birthday when a good friend of mine convinced me to start training for a marathon with him. While my buddy never made it to the starting line due to an injury, I completed my first marathon and was hooked. Over one-hundred thousand miles later, I'm still running.

While improving and competing was a priority for many years, racing and training brought a number of humorous stories along with all the miles I put in running on the roads, trails and running tracks.

The first ever marathon I ever participated in was at the Drake Relays in Des Moines, Iowa. As I stated, I was on my own for both the training and the event, as my training partner was injured and was unable to participate. I did have family support on hand at the race itself. My wife Janice and my three sons, Jason, Justin and Jonn were there to observe and cheer.

During my training, I had no "experts" to help me along. No one's experience to draw from. All the pointers I received came from reading a book put out by *"Runner's World Magazine"*.

We arrived the afternoon before the big race. I checked in at race headquarters, picked up my "race packet" and then headed to our hotel to relax. While rummaging through my packet of goodies, I came upon a map of the marathon route. "Okay", I thought, "I should probably drive the course to get the lay of the land, as to know what to expect tomorrow." So, my wife and kids piled into the station wagon, (yes, we had a station wagon in those days) found the starting line and began driving. We followed the race route as closely as possible. We came to mile one, on to mile two and then to mile three. Wow, three miles sure seemed like a long way. We forged on to mile four. E-gads! Once I got to this point tomorrow, I would still have more than twenty-two miles to go! I kept driving. At the seven-mile mark I mentally couldn't take it anymore. I was a nervous wreck! I told the family that we were heading back to the hotel. I figured I was wasting precious energy that I would need for the race. I had now developed a severe case of nerves!

The next morning I woke up at six o'clock, after getting to sleep around five o'clock. I slept very, very little through the night. I sliced up a banana and mixed it in with two packs of instant oatmeal that I warmed on a hot plate that we had brought from home. I washed it down with a bottle filled with half Gatorade and half water. I put on my racing shorts and singlet, socks and running shoes. I pinned my race number on the front of my shirt. My final bit of preparation was to slather Vaseline on my nipples (really, runners do this) and on my inner thighs and groin area to prevent the extreme pain that can come to those areas from the constant rubbing and sweating from running 26.2 miles.

It was now time to head to the family wagon and make our way toward the gold dome of the Iowa State Capital Building, where the marathon was to begin. We arrived about thirty minutes before the starting gun was to go off and found a good parking spot. Everyone in the family seemed ready to get out of the car and get the "show on the road", except for me. I was kind of hoping for a tornado sighting or some other act of God that might cancel the event. No such luck.

I eventually found just enough courage to open the car door and head towards the start area. After all, I didn't want my wife and kids thinking I was some kind of a wimp!

As I was milling around the start area, I decided to stretch a little. At least people might think I knew what I was doing. After all, that's what the majority of participants were engaged in at the time. As I looked around, all the runners looked so fast! What was I doing here? Negative thoughts began racing through my head. "I'm going to finish last?" "I'm going to have to walk a lot of this?" And the most negative of negative thoughts: "I hope I don't die out there today!"

Suddenly, out of nowhere, a runner who I figured must have been about my age came up to me and asked me a strange question. "Just exactly how far is a marathon?" "Are you kidding me?" I thought. "Twenty-six point two miles", I said. "That's a long ways: Wow!" I agreed with him and thought to myself, "I'm at least not going to finish last. Now I only had two of three negative thoughts to get out of my head!"

Shortly after this, another runner approached me. He was older and appeared, or at least gave me the impression, that he was a very experienced marathon racer. I figured he must have sensed my pending nervous breakdown and decided to strike up a conversation with me to both calm me down and shower me with his vast experience of marathon running.

My initial thought was it was nice of him to think of me, but in reality, his constant chattering had no calming effect. In fact it had just the opposite. I was literally shaking now and this guy just kept on blathering. I prayed that he'd soon just shut up and leave me alone!

For some reason, I can't explain, "Mr. Marathon" chose to start the race with me and much to my surprise and displeasure, he kept on running alongside of me. I knew he was trying to impress me with his unlimited knowledge of running. How to pace myself. How to breathe properly. How to run uphill. How to run downhill. I would just occasionally acknowledge his presence with an "uh huh" or "o.k." If I had to listen to this guy for 26.2 miles, option three of dying on the course all of a sudden didn't seem all that bad!

At the seven-mile mark on the course, a strange thing happened, that was certainly unexpected. My uninvited running partner, who had actually been quiet for a mile or so, all of a sudden blurted out: "Oh s--t! That's it. I'm done!" What? You're done? With a head full of knowledge? Your incredible experience? You're done?!? Thanks for nothing professor!

Leaving my short-term "buddy", who apparently had a bigger amount of ego than talent, was a true relief. While it didn't exactly boost my confidence, the fact that his constant yacking was no longer filling the air did take care of an unwanted annoying situation. I trudged on.

Things actually went fairly well for quite a sometime. I saw my family along the way several times which boosted my spirits, at least momentarily. Their cheering and the extra Gatorade they supplied me gave me a sorely needed bit of motivation to push me forward.

As I turned the corner near the seventeen-mile marker, I came upon two ambulances with lights flashing and a team of EMT's surrounding a runner laying prone on the hot, hard concrete of the road. "Oh my God", I thought. "A runner IS going to die here today. Out of fear and extreme fatigue, I began to make a quick evaluation of my own body. No major pain anywhere. No chest discomfort or pain in my jaws or pain working its way down my left arm. Good. I was not yet having a heart attack. I decided it was okay to continue. Less than nine miles to go!

At about mile twenty two, I noticed a runner sitting on the curb. He had removed both of his running shoes exposing two bleeding feet. He stood up, tossed his shoes off the side of the road and began running once again. He was running barefoot! He stayed ahead of me for a quarter of a mile or so, when I then passed him, never to see him again.

The last several miles were the worst case of extended discomfort (I prefer the word discomfort rather than pain) that I had ever experienced. The last two miles felt like fifteen.

I eventually made my way to the twenty-six mile mark, where I entered the beautiful Drake University Stadium and its famous blue track. There was a nice crowd on hand. I had to go just three-quarters of a lap around the track and I will have completed my first ever marathon.

And to top it off, I had run the entire way! No stops. No walking.

As I came down the final straightaway, there was a young man with wide shoulders and sporting a crew cut style haircut, approximately five yards ahead of me. I got the impression he was a Marine with his build, hair style and the totally upright way he was carrying himself. He became my main focus. Eighty yards, only a straightaway to go. I just wanted to pass him before I crossed the finish line.

I could hardly breathe and I could barely feel my legs, but it didn't matter. I now had one final goal. I accomplished that when I ended up beating "the Marine" by two steps at the finish line. I saw my family as I finished and my wife was shedding tears of joy. I'm guessing because it was all over and I was still among the living!

I was now a marathon runner. Little did I know this was just the beginning of a long running-running career?

CHAPTER 13   *Running Back to the Future*

The biggest change in the running scene since I began well over thirty years ago has been the advent of high-tech running gear, training equipment, shoes and clothing. The "science" of how to move the body more efficiently has developed and been injected into many training programs, as well.

The smallest change from what I've read, and what I've observed, is the lack of an increase in quality runners. With everything known to man to supposedly give a person every advantage, there seems to be fewer and fewer top quality runners showing up at the over-abundance of road races now available to runners.

This is not meant as a put down, just a sign of the times. Everything else in the world has gone the high-tech route, so why not running?

I thought maybe a comparison between the running scene of today and that of twenty-five or thirty years ago might be in order, just for fun.

I'd like to begin with a little discussion on clothes before we go to a cross-check comparison on a variety of other running related subjects.

In the "old days" the best runners often wore, not necessarily the worst clothes available, but seldom wore fancy, new running wear. They often wore their same "lucky" outfit, race after race and year after year. Back then, if you saw someone standing at the start line in brand new running duds, you knew you had no competitive worry from that particular runner. Seeing new, pristine clothes on other runners was a confidence builder. It meant "novice".

Not so today. Now when you head to the starting line, those who consider themselves "real runners" are milling around and warming up in the most outrageous, multi-colored, uni-sex outfits possible. Clothes that may temporarily blind you if the sun is shining brightly. But that's just the beginning.

Let's make a more detailed comparison of today's runners and those of two or three decades ago.

- CLOTHES

    Old Days---As mentioned, in the olden days the best runners often wore the worst clothing.

    Today---Best runners often look like recent graduates of The American College for Circus Performers, with multi-colored, moisture-wicking, space-age and often unflattering, form-fitting outfits.

    Old Days---Generally wore a pair of forty to fifty dollar shoes that were plain white with maybe a colored stripe or emblem on them. Plain rubber sole.

Today---Wear shoes anywhere from one-hundred to three-hundred dollars. Each shoe has somewhere between five and fifteen different colors making some male runners worried that someone may question their masculinity. Shoes come with soles filled with air, gel, helium, springs, jet packs, etc. Some even hook into computers so you can monitor your workouts in case you forgot you did one.

Old Days---Wore very short nylon shorts that when sweat-soaked, left very little to the imagination.

Today---Wear high-tech, Spandex-like, water-wicking, tight-fitting shorts that leaves very little to the imagination. Can look very good on up to approximately 15% of the women. Looks very bad on approximately 99.5% of male runners.

- EQUIPMENT

Old Days---A high percentage of the good runners didn't even wear a watch to race, but did so much running that they knew their exact pace based on "feel". At best, the runners wore a basic "sports watch" that had a "stop watch" mode on it and possibly a "lap" mode to break down the individual lap times when working out on a track. Cost: twenty to forty dollars.

Today---It's no longer a watch, it's a "training device" that costs whatever you're willing to pay for it. It comes with a heart rate monitor to make sure you know you're heart is still beating. It has an annoying pacer that beeps, LED lights and a GPS System to make sure you can find your way around the track or back to your house. Basically, it has approximately fifty modes and only two or three are truly worthwhile.

Old Days---When running in the dark, safety consisted of wearing a light colored vest with a reflective stripe or two on it.

Today---When running in the dark, you now wear a reflective vest with three to four hundred blinking LED lights and reflective tape on your arms, legs and shoes. You also need a baseball or stocking cap that comes with one or two, fifteen-hundred watt metal halide spotlights. You wear enough illumination on your body to bring a seven forty seven jet to a safe landing on any street in the city.

BASIC FACTS

Old Days---Concentrated on running smooth and easy with an upright posture and hands flowing loosely by each side of your waist. It was natural, the way God intended.

Today---Classes you pay to go to that will show you how to change what already comes naturally. Coaches introduce running techniques like "Chi" and "Pose" so you can enter a race and run the exact same time you would have if you had just saved the money and run the way nature intended instead of so uncomfortably.

Old Days---Meet your informal running club friends at 7:00 a.m. on a Saturday at a specific location to run fifteen to twenty miles and discuss future training and race plans. All at no charge.

Today---Pay one-hundred and fifty dollars to meet your formal running club friends at a specific location to run fifteen to twenty miles and discuss future training and race plans.

Old Days---There were twenty percent less marathons, but fifteen percent more sub-three hour marathoners.

Today---See above.

All said, has the all the new, extravagant equipment done much to make the sport of running better? Probably not. It all comes down to putting in the miles, dedication and putting forth maximum effort both physically and mentally.

Oh, for the "good old days"!

CHAPTER 14   *Running Math: Obsessive + Compulsive Equals?*

It's common knowledge that a high percentage of runners have obsessive-compulsive personalities. Most have their daily routines in which they feel obligated to stick to. If something comes along that forces them to eliminate their daily ritual, they tend to shake and hyper-ventilate, at least until they are able to get in some form of replacement workout. If they are totally unable to run or exercise for any reason, they may become borderline psycho. At best they function at a small percentage of their normal mental capacities.

When unable to get in a scheduled run, the brains of obsessive-compulsive runners work in a very strange way. Runners in this situation, often imagine themselves gaining at least ten pounds that day. Their ability to focus is lost. It can get so bad, that a runner who misses a workout can even have a major personality change. He or she might just become downright nasty. A person who has been one of your all-time best friends, suddenly becomes an individual you would prefer to not associate with.

I've been there. I'm one of them. I can relate. Here are a few true tales about how obsessive-compulsive I am.

In my competitive years when I had to skip a workout during the day, I would often make up for it by going to bed, trying to get a little sleep and then quietly get out of bed at two-thirty or three o'clock in the morning. I'd quickly put on my running clothes in another room, so as not to wake my wife. I'd then slip out the door and hit the streets. I remember running fifteen miles beginning at about three o'clock one Saturday morning and then coming home to get a few hours of sleep. At about eight o'clock, I then jumped up and headed out the door for a ten mile run. I have to admit, there were several occasions when I did this without anyone ever knowing. Everybody being my wife.

Missing a workout totally, was never an option for me. I always found a way.

Once, while training for the 1988 Boston Marathon, I had a twenty-three mile run scheduled on a Saturday morning. Unfortunately, the forecast called for a blizzard beginning sometime before midnight.

Instead of missing this crucial workout, I found myself at the local YMCA indoor running track at five-twenty on Friday evening. The track is short, fifteen laps to the mile, and suspended above the gymnasium floor.

Manned with a lap counter and two large bottles of a sports drink, I headed to the track with a goal of twenty-three miles or three-hundred and forty–five laps around the track!

I recruited two running friends to support me by taking "shifts" to train with me. I thought the added company would help relieve the boredom of literally running in circles for hours.

My first partner ran several miles with me early in my run, then met his family for dinner. He then came back near the end of the run and ran three more miles. In-between, another friend put in a brisk five-mile stint by my side. The two friends combined, ran a total of eleven miles with me, or nearly one half of my total distance goal. It was quite helpful and truly appreciated.

For nearly three and one-half hours, I ran around and around in circles. In my mind, it eventually became the "track from hell". "All good things (and bad things, too) must come to an end". Three-hundred and forty-five laps! I finally had done it! Three-hundred and forty-five laps? Hmmm? That's not a very round number. Three-hundred and fifty laps. Now that sounded much better! So, I ran five more laps to give me twenty-three and one third total miles. I then finished by walking one more mile just to "cool down". A grand total of three-hundred and sixty-five laps! That didn't include the times I may have forgotten to press the lap counter when I was spaced out as I began the start of another lap!

What a long evening! Talk about being stiff and sore? The next day, after struggling through five miles on my home treadmill, I was finished. I laid around the house like a slug the entire day. Folding a basket of laundry was probably my biggest contribution of the day to my family. My productivity was at a minimum!

In a similar situation on a freezing cold Saturday morning in January, I was training for the Las Vegas Half Marathon. It was three weeks until race day and I had scheduled an eighteen mile run that morning. With sleet and snow driving down outside and the temperature hovering below zero with wind chill, I decided to slip and slide to the gym in my car. Once there, I found a totally empty "cardio" room. It appeared that I was the only person crazy enough to venture out in the horrendous weather. I had the whole facility to myself.

I located my favorite treadmill, turned on a television located about ten feet in front of my machine and set two squeeze-bottles of a sports drink in the cup holders. I then set the treadmill at my desired pace. I draped a small hand towel over the display of the treadmill. By doing this, my plan was to run, and not remove the towel, until I thought I might be within a mile or two of my eighteen mile goal. I occasionally changed the incline level and adjusted the pace slightly faster or slower to simulate race conditions and to break up the monotony.

When I thought the time was right, I removed the towel. The display read seventeen and three-quarters mile. I was close. In approximately two more minutes: Bingo, goal complete!

In 1993, I was nearing the end of my training for the New York City Marathon. It was two weeks before the race and I was running a twenty-two mile run on a scenic trail near Peoria, Illinois. My wife and her friend dropped me off at the beginning of the trail and then headed towards Peoria to do some shopping.

At about the seventeen-mile mark, I felt a strange, dull pain shooting through my right groin area. Now, a "smart" person would have stopped and walked it in. Of course, I chose to keep running. I'd had minor groin strains in the past, but this didn't feel like any of the previous. Regardless, I chose to treat it as a groin injury and kept on running until I hit the end on the trail at the twenty-two mile mark.

I took it easy for a couple of days in hopes that it would just go away. It didn't. In fact, it got worse as time went on. I looked on line to try and match up symptoms with a potential diagnosis. Two or three days before we were to leave for the New York City Marathon, I unofficially concluded that I had a hernia, minus any noticeable bulge. All of the eighty-mile weeks of running, coupled with lifting progressively heavier weights three times per week, had caught up with me. My head refused to give into my body and I decided to go to New York to run the marathon, hernia or no hernia.

I had my doubts from the time I left town until I toed the starting line of the race. It was not a pleasant twenty-six mile run. From the first step, pain, numbness and a constant tingling sensation in strange places on my body were impossible to ignore, especially when it lasted for well over three hours!

I eventually made it to the finish line. I was never so happy to stop running, as I was that warm November day, when I crossed the finish line in Central Park.

Several weeks later I had surgery to repair a good old fashioned hernia, just as I had thought it was. The surgeon probably should have performed brain surgery on me instead.

Just a couple of years after the dreaded "hernia marathon", I had qualified and was training for the prestigious One-Hundredth Running of the Boston Marathon. You would think that I would have learned my lesson from the New York experience. But, wait, I'm a runner!

I have always enjoyed running on trails, especially ones that wind their way through wooded areas. There's something about running and wooded trails. I guess running is such a natural thing for humans, and to add the beauty of God's World, just enhances the total experience.

Unfortunately trails through the woods can be an evil opponent of a Boston Marathoner. I found this out first hand. My training had been going extremely well. At just three weeks before the big event, I decided to give myself a little break from the standard monotony of marathon training. I chose to run my scheduled ten-mile training run at an area state park. The trail is approximately eight and a half miles of pure, natural beauty. The paths are pretty much ungroomed, making the experience even that much better. The combination of rugged hills, rocks, trees, streams and wild life can't be beat. Unfortunately, the trail is capable of beating a runner. This particular day, it beat me.

About three miles into my run, I was day-dreaming, thinking about the upcoming marathon and about how good of shape I was in. I had hoped to run the race in under three hours, a time a very small percentage of "everyday" runners ever achieve. While I had attained the goal previously, I thought I was capable of doing one more time. I was forty-three years old and my "best days" were very close to being behind me. I was prepared mentally and physically.

As I rounded a turn in the trail, I stepped awkwardly on a rock that jutted up right in the middle of the trail. My right foot hit the rock and my ankle rolled outward about as far as a human ankle was capable of rolling. I literally heard a pop and felt sharp pain shoot through both the outside and top of my foot. I knew it was bad. I then had to hobble three pain-stricken miles back to my car.

For the next three weeks, I babied the foot. The pain eventually subsided on the side of my foot, but there was still extreme pain on the top. Marathon day was quickly approaching. I was definitely going to run the big race. Nothing was going to stop me, but I knew it probably wasn't going to be pleasant. It wasn't. I didn't obtain my time goal, but honestly I didn't care. I just wanted to see the finish line, find my family and take care of my injured foot.

Once we got back home to Iowa, I made a visit to my doctor, who scheduled an MRI of my foot. The results turned out to be exactly what I had expected. I had a stress fracture on the top of my foot. I had run the most famous running course in the world with a broken foot! I spent the next seven weeks trying to stay off my foot as much as I could. Being the obsessive-compulsive person I am, I still found a way to train for those seven weeks. I did this by "running" in the swimming pool at the local YMCA using a "water jogging belt" to keep me afloat.

I had learned my lesson. There would be no more trail runs while training for what I considered to be upcoming "important" races.

CHAPTER 15   *Runners: True Tree Tales*

I think it can safely be said that the majority of runners are a rare breed. I once read where a study conducted at a well-known university showed the average I.Q. of a large group of randomly chosen runners was significantly above the average I.Q. of athletes in other sports. Being a runner for well over thirty years, I would certainly like to believe the study to be true. Unfortunately, I do have to question the validity of the study.

After all, why would anyone want to spend hours upon hours in their lifetime sweating profusely, gasping for oxygen, injuring themselves over and over again and wearing really funny clothes? From both a physical and mental perspective, it just doesn't make good sense.

I would have to admit that spending hours on the roads, especially when running alone, allows a person time to think and reflect deeply on a variety of issues. Whether that helps in making runners more knowledgeable or just gives them a false perception that their thinking abilities are something they're really not, who knows?

There are a number of personal stories that have taken place over the years that have left me questioning not only the mental capacity, but the mental stability of runners.

This includes not only a number of stories of some of my running friends, but stories of myself, as well. For example:

In the fall of 1993, the year I turned forty, I entered a trail race near Davenport, Iowa. It was advertised as a four-mile race to be run through a scenic wooded area that was located at a youth camp.

My wife and I arrived at the race site where approximately two-hundred and fifty outdoor loving individuals were milling around, waiting to begin an exhilarating trip through nature at its finest.

Being forty years old put me into a new age grouping known as "masters". The masters division is like having a new lease on life if you're a runner. The term sounds impressive, but in reality, it just means you're now too old and too slow to compete with the young studs. But when you become a masters' runner, you run to win awards against competitors your own age and the young runners aren't eligible to win an award, even if they're miles ahead of you. They're too young!

Running is a sport where most CAN'T WAIT YO GET OLDER in order to move into a new age group of runners, who are also experiencing declining abilities. This fact alone is a case in point on the previously mentioned "I.Q study".

At this particular race I was standing around eyeing over the competition, trying to guess who was over forty years of age? I was scouting out the people I would have to be most concerned about during the race.

The race started with a literal bang from a "starter's pistol". Off went the small mass of humanity into the woods. Some of the runners were there just to be a part of the event and to do something healthy for themselves. Others like myself, were hoping to finish in the top three of the division and win a medal. I still have never quite understand why I was willing to pay twenty dollars to enter a race, another twenty-five dollars on gas and thirty dollars for a meal just to win a three dollar medal? But, as I previously stated, runners are a strange breed, as a whole. Go figure.

Off we went like a herd of deer into the dark forest. I had a plan of running right at a six minute per mile pace, somewhere around twenty-four minutes to complete the entire course.

At the two-mile marker, I was right where I had hoped to be. I was just under twelve minutes. On a trail run, accurate measurement of miles is rarely obtained. It's not uncommon for a "mile" to be twenty-five to fifty yards off due to the measuring wheel bouncing and spinning a little extra due to the rugged terrain. But I felt good and was right where I'd hoped to be.

I found myself in sixth place overall as we high-stepped deeper into the woods. I will say that there was not an overabundance of directional markers on this route. The ones I did happen to see were a dark red which tended to make them blend into the scenery. I'm certain my color-blindness didn't help matters. Honestly, I was relying on the runners in front of me to lead me to the finish line.

I continued to move smooth and easy. I remember thinking the finish should be appearing any time. I glanced over my shoulder and noticed the six of us "leaders" had made a clean break from the rest of the pack. I did see a group of runners behind us maybe forty to fifty yards. I glanced at my watch and it was approaching twenty-six minutes. It didn't feel as if my pace had slowed, but I assumed it had slightly and the course was slightly miss-measured. The finish line should be in sight any second. This was great, I thought. I was going to finish in sixth place overall, at the least, and I was positive I was the only "master" runner in the group!

We ran for several more minutes. I was getting really concerned. Could we have taken a wrong turn? Yes, we could have. Yes, we did. We meandered for another ten minutes or more. Finally I heard the sounds of the race finish area. There was music, the sounds of people chattering and an announcer over a public address system. We exited the woods and headed towards the finish line. We crossed the line in the exact opposite direction we were supposed to. I crossed the line and counted twelve more runners that finished after me. Instead of winning my age group and finishing sixth overall out of two-hundred and fifty runners, I finished in approximately two-hundred and thirty-eighth place!

By "following the leader", I had just ran approximately six miles in what was supposed to have been a four-mile race! I now better understand the disadvantages of being a "follower", not a leader. But, then again, being a leader of this race didn't exactly work out all that well, either.

While running in the woods is generally a pleasant experience, it at times can also be the location of humorous or unusual experiences, besides getting lost!

Wooded trails are a wonderful place to train with a group or by yourself. In the woods of Iowa you're pretty much safe. No lions, tigers or bears to deal with. Ticks and chiggers, poison ivy and rugged terrain constitute about ninety-nine percent of potential problems.

The biggest physical problem running on natural trails brings a runner is probably that of a sprained ankle. Over thirty-three years of running in the woods, I've probably had three or four ankles roll on me, with only one putting me on the disabled list for more than a few days. As I stated earlier, I ended up running the 1996 Boston Marathon with a stress fracture after a wicked sprain.

The "unofficial" local record for turning one's ankle on a single training run, belongs to a good friend of mine, who actually turned the same ankle three times in less than fifteen minutes. He fell to the ground writhing in pain each time. My guess is after the first fall my buddy should have wrapped up the run for the day. But, runners will be runners. After the second time, anyone else in the world would have definitely called it quits. But, three times? Something happening above the neck is just not firing on all cylinders. Keep in mind, my friend is a well-respected psychologist in the area. This guy is an expert at evaluating the human mind. He would have to charge double to evaluate himself, I guess. As amateur psychologists, we fellow runners have loved trying to evaluate him over the years, without much success. With his great sense of humor, he takes it well.

Ever notice how some people are prone to unusual experiences more than others? Our ankle turning buddy is one of those individuals. He also is the king of "off-color" jokes. I have to admit some are pretty darn good though. So maybe his higher than average "crazy" incident rate is God's little payback for his "not so good" jokes.

On another training run, in the same woods, our small group was moving along smoothly on one of our favorite trails. We came upon what was normally a small stream that we typically crossed by tip-toeing over some large rocks on the bed of the stream. This allowed us to end up back on the trail on the opposite side of the stream.

Several days prior to this run we had experienced exceptionally heavy rains. Soft trails were not our problem, as we were accustomed to that. This time, the rains were so long and hard, that it caused our little stream to develop into a fast moving, small river of approximately three feet in depth.

The "flood" had swept a mass of tree branches, bushes and small logs directly on our rock path, making it virtually impossible to cross to our beloved trail.

The group chose to forget trying to cross the stream that day, except for one person. Our joke-telling, ankle twisting, high I.Q. friend decided he could take care of the situation, with or without help. We decided he was on his own.

Like a human tornado, he began removing branches and brush. I have to admit he was doing a remarkable job. After a few minutes, a fairly good size log was revealed. Access to the log would allow him to cross the water further and hopefully finish cleaning up the job. We could then use the log to cross the stream as a group and continue on our originally planned route. I was truly impressed with his work. In fact, I was preparing to praise his efforts and enthusiasm, when he looked back at the group and started to say something profound, I'm sure. It was then, he slipped on the log and proceeded to fall head first into the water. Eventually we saw just two feet, sporting soaked running shoes, emerging from the water. He soon regained his sense of direction, righted himself and stood up in the water. He was fortunately, unscathed. If he was embarrassed, he certainly didn't show it. In fact he was talking a blue streak as soon as his mouth came out of the water.

It was a warm day, thank goodness. In fact, after he crossed to the other side and stood on the running path, the rest of us gingerly made our way over the log and completed the run we had originally set out to do. We didn't let our soggy buddy hear the end of his "fall from grace" episode until we were finished and he had gotten into his car to head home.

One final "running in the woods" story. This story edges towards a "PG-13" rating, so if you have children reading this book, you might want the pages of this story to magically disappear.

I was running in a park on a beautiful late October afternoon. I was training for the upcoming St. Louis marathon. The course was a rugged route around a gorgeous lake. Hills, streams and wildlife made it one of the most enjoyable runs in the area.

I was nearing the finish of the run with a little less than one mile to go. I came upon a small clearing, where I would have to cross a park road to connect up to the trail, located just on the other side. I was about to step on the road, when I heard some unusual sounds coming from a small hillside to my left. Upon a closer look, I saw a young couple who obviously had a strong affection for each other. Let's just say they were enjoying more than just a picnic in the woods.

The couple was no more than twenty-five feet from the main trail and basically in plain sight to the world. Oddly, by coincidence, it must have been both the girl and the guy's birthday that day, as they both were lying in the grass in their "birthday suits".

They seemed to be enjoying their party immensely. It was definitely a private party.

I have to admit, I did slow down slightly just to be sure I was seeing what I thought I was seeing. Really, that was the only reason! I was right.

There was no cake, no candles, but definitely a big display of fireworks!

I hope the chiggers, ticks and poison ivy weren't out in full force that afternoon. Any of these could have put a real damper on a great party.

CHAPTER 16 *Runners---Personality Question Marks*

Runners are unquestionably a collectively unique bunch. No two runners are the same. Each has a personality that is theirs' and theirs' alone. Personalities run the gauntlet of extremes. Running seems to bring out the best in some runners, while just the opposite is true in others. There are some poor souls that running even brings out the "Sybil" in them, in the form of multiple personalities!

You can find runners that are, most definitely, highly intellectual when you spend time on the roads with them. Others seem to hover on the edge of "lunatic fringe". Fatigue and hormones often appear be factors that may help in defining many runners' personality traits.

One former "intellectual" (Who unfortunately, I'm sadden to say, passed away just a few years ago) rarely brought up the subject of running when running. He held a doctoral degree in psychology. He was one of my favorite running partners. We discussed "deep" subjects on a regular basis when running together. Our conversations had a wide range of topics that varied from classical music to jazz on one run, to medicine and psychology on another day's run. Over the years we discussed politics, religion and even sex, in detail. I always felt like a more knowledgeable person after completing a run with this wonderful friend. I miss him.

Another great friend and running partner who is also a "Brainiac" in his own right, used training runs as an outlet from the "real world" and spent ninety percent of our training runs talking about, well---running. Upcoming races, past races, training methods and nutrition were our main focus. It was always a pleasure exchanging running notes and swapping running and racing stories.

Both of the friends I mentioned, were men I always looked forward to running with, regardless of their differences of conversation on the road. Both were pleasant, humorous and dedicated to their ultimate goal. That was to become better runners. They both accomplished their mission.

An all-time favorite running companion of each and every member of our running group was a "one-of-a-kind". No one else was had similar traits. You never knew what to expect from him, but I would put a twenty dollar bill on it, each and every time we were to run, that the subject of food would dominate a fairly large share of his conversation.

Conversation often began with what he food he over-indulged in the night before and then turned to what he had to eat in preparation for the run he was about to undertake. Once on the run, dialogue swayed to the planned or potential breakfast we as a group might be sharing together once the run was over. The food he ate prior to arriving to our training run never seemed to count as a "real" breakfast.

Lunch and dinner plans and possible menu items for later in the day were often filtered in to the discussion.

Interspersed between all this talk of food was often a vocal concert of some of the world's greatest all-time rock and roll oldies sang in a totally new manner that world has yet to appreciate.

This guy was energetic and loved by all. He was so entertaining and on top of it all, he was an excellent runner. One of the best in our motley little crew, he made running fun!

Discussion is generally a good thing in group runs. It helps to pass the time and can be entertaining or educational.

On the negative side, there are the occasional runners who seem to have personalities that tend to change as the miles mount. From my experience, when a runner's personality swings in a different direction, the changes are often not for the best.

One woman runner, who was a very good runner, actually seemed to have multiple personalities. As the miles increased, personality changes followed. There seemed to be a direct correlation between miles run and changes in personality. I would call this woman the "Sybil" of our running group. The farther she went, the more dramatic and noticeable the changes became. Not being a medical professional, I can only guess that a combination of fatigue and hormones come together to form some sort of magical mood swing(s). I would have to say it was extremely entertaining to watch.

When this woman began a run, she was a pleasure to be around. She was funny, talkative and animated. As the miles increased, the positives seemed to fade accordingly.

Somewhere around the eight-mile mark of the run, chatter, wittiness and good humor turned abruptly, one-hundred and eighty degrees. She seldom spoke unless spoken to.

Mile eight was the magic mark where the Jekyll and Hyde syndrome made its appearance. A simple question, such as: "How are you doing?" often brought about an immediate display of anger. The answer came with words that are best kept from the ears of children. I'm pretty sure this nice lady was never a sailor, so there had to be a logical explanation.

The best solution was quite simple. Don't ask the woman how she's doing until the run was completed. This what the group chose to do---with one exception.

This particular runner, who was known as a prankster, a joke-teller and an instigator (he's been mentioned previously more than once) was just looking for trouble and seemed to thrive on it.

"Sympathy" and "compassion" were not in his vocabulary in this instance. "Irritation"? Now that's another story. There's was no mercy and he did his best (I will admit he was extremely proficient at this) to bug the heck out of this poor woman.

A few words by this master of psychology sent this petite woman runner into a state of emotional instability that I can only say is "you have to be there to appreciate". The poor woman would often yell rather choice words at a rapid-fire rate which only fueled the instigators' fire to continue his less than subtle harassment. The back and forth barrage of words continued until the run was complete.

Another running friend had personality changes similar to our lady running club member. He, however needed no human prompting. He just needed the miles. More miles than our lady friend, but with similar results.

I had never noticed this until he committed to training his first full-length marathon. He asked me to run and assist with his training, which I gladly did. Personally, I've always loved the long (twenty miles or more) training runs that are such an important part of marathon training. This, however, was his first venture in running a single continuous run of twenty miles or more.

Our "virgin marathoner" was following the training schedule I had designed for him to a tee. He had steadily progressed to longer mileage having completed a sixteen-miler two weeks earlier. He completed the run with relative ease.

Now it was time to increase the long run to eighteen miles. He was handling it very well, until about mile sixteen. The last two miles became filled with consistent complaining, but nothing really out of the ordinary.

Fourteen days later was the "big day". His first twenty-mile run. The twenty-miler is always a milestone for a distance runner. I can state with certainty, he was pumped and ready to go!

At mile seventeen, the complaints aggressively began. "My legs are getting numb", "this is a really a long, freakin' way to run", and "I'm getting a blister on my right foot." These words were nothing I hadn't heard before. For that matter, I've said them to myself many times over the years. But from mile eighteen to the completion of the run at mile twenty, it was a different story. The complaints became major, followed by a slew of four-letter words, all at a very high decibel level. Anyone walking on the sidewalk or living in a home on the street we were running on, may very well have entertained thoughts of calling in law enforcement officers.

I spent most of the last two miles trying to run far enough ahead or behind my buddy, hoping people wouldn't think I knew him.

We completed the twenty-mile run and walked it off. There was very little complaining during the cool down period. Instead, pride of accomplishment set in. His talk was lively and upbeat.

It's pretty amazing how achieving ones' goal that was once thought impossible can change a persons' demeanor from downright nasty, to excited and proud.

One final running story to prove my point that runners may fall somewhere close to the cross-over line of sane and insane.

Running in Burlington, Iowa in the early nineties was at its' peak. There were more good runners pounding the pavement than any time before and since. The city had two runners who had run full-length marathons under two hours and thirty minutes and at least five others who had ran well under three hours. It was the last years of the "running boom" created by the earlier success of running greats Frank Shorter, Bill Rodgers and Steve Prefontaine.

It was the middle of the morning on New Year's Eve Day. The temperature was in the low to mid- twenties. It was a bit breezy and it was spitting a light snow. In those days we considered it a perfect day for putting in a thirteen-mile run. Four seasoned runners met me at my house to begin the jaunt through this holiday winter wonderland.

Three of the five runners were sub-three hour Boston Marathoners, another runner had finished third right behind Frank Shorter in a ten-mile race a couple of years before, thus proving he was quite an accomplished runner, as well.

The fifth runner might have had the most "raw" talent of us all, and had even raced a couple of decent races in the past. He chose, however, to do the majority of his hard work in training. While the rest of us chose to train to race, runner number five generally trained to train. Top notch conditioning seemed to be his ultimate goal. He spent much of his training beating the rest of the runners in town into oblivion.

He was one of a few at that time who incorporated technology into his workouts. He might have been the first in the area to use a heart rate monitor in an attempt to improve himself as a runner.

He was a true obsessive-compulsive, who had little flexibility when it came to changing up his routine. In fact, when he and I would run together, we would run the same eight-mile route day after day. To alleviate any possible mental breakdowns, I incorporated the sacred eight-mile route into the thirteen-miler planed for our holiday group run.

Once runner number five adjusted his heart rate monitor and hit the button, we were off. The course soon found its' way to a local park, where at the two mile mark, our "set in his ways" runner ALWAYS had to make a "pit stop". He would stop and hide behind the same bush, day after day, week after week and month after month. Nothing different this day. Standard procedure for a stop like this, is for the other runners in the group to jog slowly around the area while waiting for the indisposed runner to finish his business.

Our group of four "waiters" had already expected the stop and made a decision not to wait on number five. We had pre-planned to take off at a quick pace of about six minutes per mile and keep it up for two to three miles. We all knew that "number five" wouldn't have the patience to wait for us to slow down allowing him to catch up with us. We were certain if we were running a six-minute mile, he would run closer to a five-minute pace in an attempt to reel us in. We were right!

So off we went, leaving our poor buddy "in the dust" or snow in this case. We had a very substantial lead when we looked back and saw our flustered friend in hot pursuit.

We gradually eased off some to allow him to gain on us a little quicker. It was still somewhere between two and three miles before he finally was able to close the gap.

The funny thing that stands out in my mind, had to do with the heart rate monitor he was wearing. He always set the monitor in the "perfect" range for his runs. If he ran too slowly, it would annoyingly beep, loud and continuously. This signaled to him that his heartrate was too low and he needed to pick up his pace to receive full benefits. If his heart rate was over the suggested maximum rate for the run, the monitor would do the same, reminding him to slow down the pace in order to stay out of oxygen debt.

When he was within about a quarter of mile of us, the wind must have been blowing in the perfect direction, as we could all hear his heart monitor beeping like crazy. He was above the max and breathing loudly and quickly. He was also sweating like a man just exiting a steam room. When he finally caught us, he was totally spent. In fact, this was one of the few times we ever saw him actually stop running and have to walk, which he had to do several times before completing the thirteen-mile run. It was a nasty trick on our part.

Isn't wonderful to have such great and caring friends. Runners are like that.

CHAPTER 17   *Shine or Rain---It's Only Pain*

Athletes of old were known to play through injuries and pain. It would take being run over by a freight train to keep the great competitors of yesteryear out of a line-up. Even then, if the train didn't break any bones, it was highly likely the athlete would still do whatever they could to play that day.

Major League pitchers often pitched nine innings or more, often suffering from small rotator cuff tears or severe elbow strains. On three days of rest, they were back in a game doing it all over again.

The same held true for professional football and basketball players. Despite lower quality training facilities and medical aid, athletes played with fractures, tears, sprains and strains. They would do anything to stay in the line-up of the game they loved.

Not so much today. For example, Major League pitchers typically throw five or six innings and then are replaced by fresh hurlers. If a small blister appears on the pinkie of their non-throwing hand or there's a tiny twinge in any body part, they're put on a fifteen-day disabled list.

Understandably, baseball (and major sports as a whole) have become a ridiculously lucrative entertainment business and owners feel obligated to protect their grossly overpaid investments.

Give me a break! With all the high-tech fitness equipment, year around workouts, nutritionists to go along with super mind and body specialists, wouldn't you think the athletes of today should be able to play the majority of a season without major injury? Good grief, Bob Gibson pitched thirteen complete game shutouts in one season back in the late sixties for the St. Louis Cardinals.

It seems the modern athlete lives in a culture that coddles and pampers them to a point of extreme. Guaranteed multi-million dollar contracts contribute to make the situation even worse. Players know they are going to be paid regardless if they play or not. Does this take away motivation to perform well day after day? Whatever happened to playing for the simple love of the game?

I know there are still players who play because they have a passion for the game. It does appears to be the exception, not the rule. Fewer and fewer players play for the original reason the game was invented in the first place; it's just plain fun! Personally, in my day (in fact, even today) I would play for absolutely nothing just to be able to put on a major league uniform.

Running the 1993 New York City Marathon with an extremely painful hernia was not a pleasant experience. But, I ran it! Point to be made? Nothing was going to stop me from running that race. I loved to run and I had pride in the blood, sweat and tears I had put in to get myself there.

I would deal with the health consequences when it was over. No fifteen day disabled list for me, at least until I could say "I've done it." I completed and ran the New York City Marathon, hernia or no hernia.

A similar experience happened at the 100th Running of the Boston Marathon in 1996. I had qualified to run this race at the Chicago Marathon in the fall of 1994 and I was pumped and ready to train hard and do well.

On a Saturday, two weeks and two days before the race, I made the incredibly dumb mistake of planning my last "long run" on the ungroomed trails of a local state park. My plan was to run and enjoy the trees, the wildlife and nature in general.

I was excited knowing this would be the culmination of a long, hard training schedule. I was excited about this run, because, when completed, I would begin the part of training every marathoner cherishes---"the taper". An informational side note: the taper consists of shorter, slower, easy runs and a day or two completely off. This allows the body to recover and repair from weeks of fine-tuning, preparing it to run as fast as it can for 26.2 miles.

I arrived at the parks' trail head just after sunrise, my favorite time of all to run. After a brief warm-up and some light stretching, I took off. Approximately three miles into the run, I made a sharp turn on the trail. This is where the "incredibly dumb plan" became reality.

This was an ungroomed trail which included sticks, water, leaves, ruts and rocks of all sizes and shapes. Some of these rocks (well, at least one) happened to be hidden under leaves. I certainly found this rock by mistake! I stepped on the side of it and my right ankle turned outward violently. I heard a pop and immediately fell to the ground writhing in pain. It felt serious. I looked down and saw the ankle and top of my foot was already swelling to enormous proportions. Definitely not good.

My very first thought was, "Oh no, no Boston Marathon!" I couldn't believe it. "What am I going to do now? Should I continue to run and see if my ankle begins to loosen up?" I quickly realized that would definitely not be the smart thing to do.

I started hobbling (mostly hopping on my "good" foot) back to my car. After what seemed like an eternity, I arrived at the vehicle and headed home. I made a quick stop at a convenience store to pick up a bag of ice to begin my therapy.

I had just over two weeks to heal before the big race. I made the decision I was NOT calling a doctor until after the race. I had a pretty good idea of what he would tell me if I did see him. I was not going to miss the 100th running of the world's most prestigious marathon.

For the next fifteen days I quit running totally, stayed off my foot as much as possible, iced it, and went through two bottles of ibuprofen.

On Patriots Day in Boston, I stood at the starting line with what was still a very sore, very swollen foot. The gun went off and within a few steps, intense pain shot through my right foot and ankle. Only 26.2 miles to go! The pain was excruciating until about mile sixteen or seventeen when I noticed my right foot had gone numb. I hobbled another ten miles to the finish line and was actually quite surprised how fast I arrived there considering the condition I was in.

When we arrived home a couple of days later, I made an appointment with my doctor. After examination and a test or two, it was determined I had been trying to heal a major stress fracture for the past three weeks. Running a marathon on it certainly didn't help in the healing process.

I was told no running for seven weeks straight. I followed doctor's orders and stayed in shape by treading water in a swimming pool while wearing a "jogging belt". I did this every day for forty-nine days straight.

So why did I run a marathon with a broken bone in my foot? Obsessive-compulsive behavior? Without a doubt. Not giving in after months and months of dedication and discipline? Most certainly. A pure love of the sport? That was the number one reason! To think I didn't even have a multi-year multi-million dollar contract!

CHAPTER 18   *Senior Moments--- Athletic Style*

Competitive sports for most athletes come to an end by around age forty. After four decades, the body tends to show the wear and tear of years competition, of practice, multiple injuries and Mother Nature just doing the things she just does naturally to the human body. Many athletes also begin to lose that "competitive fire" that burned intensely inside them for so long. There's a mind set to some of the "old schoolers" that people in their forties and beyond are just too old to be playing games. Staying physically and mentally fit is of utmost importance to many of the forty and over crowd, but competing should be a thing of the past.

There is, however, a "select" group of men who come together for one week every year in the warm desert sun of Las Vegas, Nevada, to compete in the National 50 and 60 and Over Baseball Championships. These unique, talented, individuals shred that "no competitive sports after the age of forty" stereotype to bits. They break away from their everyday work or retirement activities, in exchange for a colorful baseball uniform.

They put on metal-cleated baseball shoes, carry bags filled with $200.00 baseball bats and $150.00 baseball gloves to play "America's Pastime".

They are no longer middle-aged men or senior citizens. They become magically transformed into "The Boys of Summer" (or in this case, "The Boys of Fall"). They are ready to spend a week playing the game they love. Each and every one of the members of the twenty-plus teams begin the week in hopes of playing on the following Saturday for the right to claim the title of "National Champion".

A good share of these teams have been together for many, many years, having played in leagues and/or other tournaments around the country. Some are league champions, while others may be league "all-star" teams. Regardless of how they got together, the teams are filled with talented, competitive, fifty to seventy-year-old athletes who play their hardest and give one-hundred percent. There are generally even a few former major league players scattered throughout the rosters.

One might expect this tournament to be filled with a bunch of slow-moving, overweight men. But this is not an "old-timers" tournament. Sure, some of the players might be a touch thicker around the middle than they were thirty or forty years before, but typically, not much. These guys work hard at staying in top physical condition and put in the time to keep their playing skills honed.

They're fun-loving athletes who are determined to play their best. The great thing is, they put the whole experience into perspective. Winning is a priority, but they also realize that losing is just as much part of the game. Bad experiences and memories are brief and soon forgotten. Losses are washed from the mind quickly.

Tomorrow is a new day and looked forward to with renewed enthusiasm and optimism.

On game days, if a player is scheduled to play at 8:00 a.m., he typically rises early, dresses for the game, eats a light breakfast and is then off to one of a number of highly manicured baseball fields in around the Las Vegas area. By 7:30 a.m., he is on the field playing catch, taking infield and outfield practice and getting in a few practice swings with the bat. At 8:00 a.m. the players are mentally and physically ready to rock and roll; looking to make a positive impact for their team.

The games played that week are filled with a very high level of baseball. Exciting defensive gems, pinpoint pitching, perfect bunts and even the occasional fence-clearing long ball. Physical errors are rare and mental mistakes pretty much non-existent.

While a fifty to seventy year-old human body can be kept in amazing condition, it does have its' limitations. The first game of the week generally produces an injury or two per team. Hamstrings, quadriceps and calf muscles seem to dominate the list. The pain is eased later in the day with ice packs, ibuprofen and whirlpools. Often a players' drink of choice provides temporary relief, as well.

As the week progresses so does the total number of the "walking wounded". Each day the hotel whirlpools become more and more crowded. By weeks' end, a player almost needs to take a number to get a coveted spot in the warm, swirling waters.

Come "Championship Saturday", if a team has two players still injury free, it's unusual. Regardless of the injuries, there's no holding back. Players will "play through" their injury or injuries to play for a wooden plaque that tells everyone they are a baseball "National Champion". The players' theory is that once the tournament is over, they'll have all the time necessary to recover and let their battered bodies heal.

One of my most exciting weeks---EVER---took place in October of 2006. On Friday evening, I watched my beloved St. Louis Cardinals defeat the Detroit Tigers to win the World Series. The next morning at 8:00 a.m., I was playing for a 60 and Over National Championship, as one of the two "underage" players allowed to play on a team to fill out a teams' roster. We won! At 11:00 a.m., I was on another field vying for a 50 and Over National title. Once again, the team I was playing for (a team headquartered out of New England) won. In a period of about nineteen hours, my favorite major league team became World Champion and I had won two national baseball championships. It couldn't have been a better finish to a fantastic week!

Once the champions are crowned and the final team photos are snapped, many of the players often have one more night in Vegas before catching their flight home the next day. The final evening is filled with players from many of the teams getting together for one last meal or drink. The dinner table or bar is filled with reminiscing and final goodbyes. It's the end of a terrific week.

What's the main difference between professional baseball and 50/60 and Over Baseball? Over 50/60 ball players have to pay to play. There are no multi-million dollar contracts. These players are, however, just as thrilled to be champions. They play for pure love of the game!

Section 3
(Stories from a Coach)

CHAPTER 19   Tee Ball by the Numbers

Coaching youth can be one of the most rewarding undertakings you'll ever encounter. It can also be one of the most taxing and frustrating experiences on the face of the planet.

Coaching five and six year olds and attempting to familiarize them to our "National Pastime" is a crazy world all to itself.

You would think teaching kids the basics of the game would be moderately easy but, trust me, that's not the case. Thank goodness these "miniature" athletes only have to learn to hit a stationary ball sitting on a tee, as opposed to a ninety-mile per hour fastball moving through the air.

One definite positive is five and six year olds tend to have an over-abundance of energy and enthusiasm. On the negative side, young children typically lack the patience and the ability to focus for any extended length of time. Their little minds are lucky to be able to concentrate on any one thing longer than (I'm being generous here) thirty seconds consecutively. With this said, a good tee ball coach must work quickly and efficiently. However, with ten to fifteen "tee-ballers", concentration and focus ability of the entire team in general drops in direct relationship to the total number of kids present. This means teaching must be well thought out in advance if there's going to be any actual learning taking place for these true "Boys (and Girls) of Summer".

Baseball is a game dominated by statistics. Batting, fielding, pitching; there's a corresponding number that lets the whole world know how you compare to everyone else who plays the game. In tee ball, no one is concerned about stats.

However, after coaching three different tee-ball teams over the years, I've come up with some tee-ball stats of a little different type. This is an unscientific study, but I think the following percentages are somewhat accurate. Like political polls, I give these stats a plus or minus four percent swing either way. So, here is "tee-ball by the numbers" from one guys' perspective:

- Approximately thirty-three and a third percent of the players will start their first practice of the season with their fielders' glove on the wrong hand.
- Generally around fifty percent will come up to bat the first time with their hands crossed on the bat.

- Close to twenty-five percent of all batters will face the wrong direction on their first attempt to hit during their teams' first practice.
- Conservatively, eighty-eight percent of the players will swing and completely miss the ball on the first swing they take at practice. They will either swing above the ball or pound the heck out of the poor rubber tee.
- Once players start making contact with the ball and are allowed to run for the first time, only about twenty percent will run to first base, as the rule states they should. Thirty-five percent will make a mad dash to third base instead and a whopping forty-five percent make a beeline towards second base.
- Unfortunately, thirty percent of the players will cry before the first practice ends, breaking the well-known unwritten rule of, "there's no crying in baseball!"
- You can count on this one. The first time the team plays a real game and someone from the other team hits a fair ball, all but two of the defensive players will converge on the ball. Basically all will be fighting over who gets to pick it up and throw it. The other two players will not move because they were not paying attention and didn't even know the ball was hit! They were instead picking dandelions.

During game situations, there are a number of things that are a given. Including:

- An airplane flying overhead will temporarily put the game on hold.
- The playing field will be virtually dandelion free by games' end.
- At least one parent will question an umpire's call during the game. Really? Who cares?
- At least one parent will unofficially keep score during the game. Really? Who cares?
- Two to three players will call time out sometime during the game in order to use the restroom.
- Every game will find a minimum of two occurrences where more than one player of the offensive team is standing on the same base.
- Even if the final score is forty-five to one, no player will question which team won if you just say the game ended in a tie.
- At least one player will get hurt at games' end while rushing to the "treat cooler" for their post-game snack.

When you think about it, who really deserves a multi-million dollar contract to coach, a major league manager or a tee-ball coach? I can tell you which job is by far the tougher of the two.

CHAPTER 20 *the Traveling Team Dilemma*

There's an old saying in youth sports that in summary says: keep adults from being involved in sports for kids and everything will be great. After all, games were in most cases first created for kids to enjoy the movement and the competition that comes with them.

Let the kids play the game, don't allow adults to coach, officiate, administrate or even spectate, and things will work out just fine.

Of course, without adults, (the right adults) kids wouldn't have much chance to develop their skills (both physically and mentally) to the fullest. Unfortunately, poor coaches often take away from what the game was originally designed for: FUN!

From my many, many years of coaching, it is my opinion that there is a fair percentage of adults in coaching these days that really shouldn't be. Before I go on, let me make it clear that there are also many very fine coaches.

When it comes to the lower tier of coaches, many lack the knowledge of the finer points of the game, some are just plain poor teachers and others don't relate well with the age group they're coaching. There are others who are in the game looking to promote their kid's own glory, as opposed to building the skill sets of all the kids they coach. Find a coach who possesses more than one of these deficiencies and it's pretty much a given the children are in for a bad experience. There are, of course, those wonderful people who volunteer to coach because no one else will. In this case the experience can go either way; but, at least, they will give it their best shot.

The "traveling team" is now the big thing when it comes youth sports. A good thing or bad? I have been able to see many players preparing to join their high school teams after playing forty games with their traveling squads. Parents of these players often come to the high school team coaching staff, to proudly let the coaches know that their child has been a member of one of these "elite" teams. The poor parent thinks because they've just spent hundreds of dollars and enormous chunks of time for their kid to participate on one of these teams, their child is now the second coming of Ted Williams.

From personal experience, this is about as far from reality as it gets. While there are the occasional standouts that come from the traveling teams, it looks to be the exception rather than the rule. In these cases I often think these top players would have been a star regardless whether they played for the traveling team or not. Quite honestly, prior to the traveling team explosion, teams as a rule, were more fundamentally sound defensively, offensively and maybe even more so mentally, than the teams of today.

Here's an example of the sometimes skewed thinking of the poor parent who thinks the only way their kid will be able to compete at a high level in the future, is to participate on a traveling team today.

About eight or nine years ago, I was coaching as an assistant for our local high school team. The school is considered one of the larger schools in the state. There are four classes of schools: 1A, 2A, 3A and 4A with 1A being the smallest of schools and 4A the largest. We had established ourselves as an annual 4A power, having had a winning record year after year. To play on our high school team, a boy had to be a good, solid, all-around player. One day, I was stopped in a store by a former player I had coached a number of years before. He was an above-average player in his day. Since that time, he had become a father. His boy was eight years old at the time of our conversation.

His son was now playing on a newly formed "traveling team" which the former player was helping to coach. As we talked, his conversation turned to a serious lecture on how coaches (including myself) should be coming out on weekends to "scout" the elite traveling squads. His theory was that we coaches would then know the talent that would be coming our way in the years to come. This guy's eight year old was one of the standouts on the team. I'm sure he thought we would then be licking our chops waiting for his little slugger to reach high school age, where he could then carry us to a state championship.

I politely listened to him, occasionally shaking my head in what was nothing more than a polite gesture. There was no way. I might go watch the occasional game, but as a fan of baseball, and only then if I really had nothing else to do that day.

Eight year old stars are often turn out to be seventeen year old average players. Average and even below average eight year olds grow. Some blossom as athletes. They may become much stronger and faster. They may become dedicated to the sport and put in extra work. They may have a better coach or coaches somewhere between ages eight and seventeen that make them stronger all-around players with fewer weaknesses. In other words, a dominant player at eight, certainly is no indication of what type of player he will be eight to ten years down the road. The eight year old who had may not even made the team, may someday be the All-State player, who ends up with the "full ride" scholarship to college.

Back to the father and his son. Eight or nine years later, the onetime stud ended up playing for a small high school. He was one of the two or three better players on the team. While he may have possibly made the team for a large school, he would certainly have had limited playing time.

Personally, I think a child is better off spending time with a proven coach, taking private lessons and making sure his fundamentals are solid.

Traveling teams? Enjoy them for what they are, a chance for kids to get to play the great game of baseball. They are not a stepping stone to future greatness as so many have come to believe.

CHAPTER 21 *How to Lead by Example---Not!*

Little League baseball was created back in the 1950's for young boys age eight to twelve. It was to give them a healthy, competitive and enjoyable outlet to not only play America's National Pastime, but to learn life-long traits such as discipline, respect, teamwork and dedication.

To make this happen, the program would need adults throughout the United States to lead each local chapter. These are the people who would be charged with carrying out these important expectations.

To be successful, each program would need caring, understanding and knowledgeable adults. Mature individuals able to lead by example. Adults who would pass positive traits along to the young athletes they would be dealing with.

Since the fifties, the adult role model has been prevalent throughout Little League baseball. There have been and there are many today, who have developed terrific programs and been outstanding leaders, as well as ultimate role models.

The problem is that for every ten nearly perfect role models in youth sports, there's always one or two "knuckleballs", masquerading as coaches or administrators. There are the glory-seekers, the power hungry and the former athletic failures who find that coaching youth is a way to achieve the recognition that may have eluded them in sports.

Let me relay a true story that I had some involvement that accurately defines the above term of "knuckleball".

I was coaching a team in Little League baseball. It was a "minor league" team; which means the majority of the kids playing were eight or nine years old. It was just minutes before game time.

I was speaking to the team who was anxiously sitting on the bench. I was reviewing signals and trying my hardest to motivate a team that had been somewhat lethargic during warm-ups.

As I was speaking, I noticed another coach and the president of the league were having a discussion directly behind our dugout. Behind them, was a second playing field. Another game was also about to begin on that diamond. With the way the two fields were positioned, it happened that there was another team of youngsters in a dugout squarely behind ours. Only about fifteen feet separated the two dugouts with the coach and president having their discussion midway between the two benches. They were so close, that the players from both teams could almost touch them.

So, between approximately thirty young boys stood the two adult "leaders" in a long discussion that was only getting longer and what appeared to be more intense.

I noticed as the conversation progressed, the volume of their voices was gradually increasing. It was obvious things were beginning to heat up. I kept on talking to my team, all the while keeping one eye on our team and one eye zeroed in on the two men.

Out of the blue, the coach lunged at the league president with enough force that the president did everything he could to avoid ending up on the ground. The nimble president quickly regained his balance and immediately shot his body straight into the coach. It was like a football lineman putting s block on a cornerback. It was definitely on! Several free-swinging fists flew from both participants with none fortunately hitting the intended mark with any precision. The brawl then turned from a poor version of amateur boxing into an even poorer example of free-style wrestling. As the two kept up their battle, both men were adding words to the heated dispute that wouldn't be welcome in a college locker room.

I quickly sprinted through the dugout, having cut my team speech short. I reluctantly put my body between the two "grown men". Fearing that I might be the one who would be seriously injured, the two combatants eventually began to regain their composure. Both men were realizing what they had just done and were obviously embarrassed by the thirty or so pairs of young eyes that were focused on them in total disbelief.

Eventually, with no apologies from either party, the two "leaders" stepped back and went in different directions. Both were sporting a combination of anger and embarrassment as they slithered away.

I felt both should be men enough to apologize to the kids who had just witnessed this human eruption of emotions, but neither did. I ended up being the one who apologized for them.

A shining example of perfect role models, it was not. For five to ten minutes that evening, it was nearly impossible to determine who the adults were and who the kids were. This type of thing happens way too often in the world of youth sports.

CHAPTER 22   More Adults We Can Do Without

From my experience, many parents seem to think their own children are much more accomplished at whatever sport they participate in than they actually are.

So many parents are under the impression that spending half their life savings on equipment, uniforms, equipment bags, entry fees, and fuel and motel expenses is the magic formula for athletic success. The way to get their young athlete into the "hall of fame" someday. It has come to my attention, way too many of these uninformed parents are often clueless in term of the benefits, or lack thereof, their investment brings.

As I mentioned earlier, I'm not a big fan of traveling teams. My personal experience has shown the perceived benefits parents expect, very seldom come true. From my standpoint, the reasons are many, including:

- Lack of proper fundamentals being taught by a high percentage of coaches.
- Burn-out of kids from too many games and practices at such a young age. Too much of anything can kill enthusiasm.
- The exceptionally high expenses for parents whose children are involved.

- Specialization of one sport at an age. Kids should be experiencing a variety of sports to become a better-rounded athlete.
- The time a sport takes away from the family doing important things together. For instance, church is becoming a thing of the past for many families, as tournaments are generally held on weekends. There appears to be no regards as to what is truly important in life, especially for young children.

You can blame the adults, some who appear to be wearing blinders. It seems they succumb to peer pressure to get their kids on these teams. In their minds, if their child is to have any chance to compete at a high level, some six to ten years down the line, the traveling team is the answer.

As a high school assistant baseball coach, our team had a player whose father never missed his son's game. The player, a former "traveling teamer", had average talent. He was good enough to make the team, but with limited abilities. He was not a star, but more of a role-type player, filling in where needed. The player did pitch on occasion, but was by no means dominate. He generally lasted only a few innings per game at best, on a "good day". The coaching staff was aware of the player's deficiencies, Dad, however, was not. The father virtually believed his son was the second coming of Nolan Ryan.

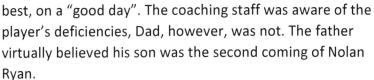

Each and every game "junior" took the mound, Dad positioned himself directly behind home plate armed with a very expensive, self-purchased "JUGS" radar gun! The same type of gun major league scouts use to measure the velocity of major league pitchers and prospects.

Dad would "clock" each and every pitch, often signaling to his son with a "thumbs up" or giving hand signals to indicate where he thought his son should throw the next pitch.

Again, the coaches could see the kid was not an outstanding pitcher. Decent speed, but not over-powering. No really good off-speed pitch and control problems of a high magnitude. Take all this and add to it the pressure the father put on his son to perform and you could see "failure" written all over it, for a truly good kid.

Personally, I always wanted to take the radar gun and measure how fast we could get dad to run to his car and head home.

Traditionally our high school baseball team played a doubleheader (two seven inning games) most game days. The typical routine was that with a twenty-five to thirty minute break between games, I would quickly head to the concession stand to get the head coach and myself a soft drink and a hot dog. These healthy treats were to give us a little additional "nutrition" to get us through the second game.

I would conservatively guess that ten times in my career, I was stopped by a "concerned" parent, looking for answers to such important questions as: "Why isn't my son getting more playing time?" Or maybe: "How come my son is batting seventh instead of third?" Another popular inquiry was: "It's been two weeks since my boy pitched. Is he ever going to pitch again?"

Being the assistant coach, it was my duty to direct all questions to the head coach. I have to admit, I would have loved to answer many of the questions the parents were afraid to ask the head coach in the first place! Answers such as: "Sorry your son isn't playing, but he's hitting .175 and has committed fourteen errors in the last eight games." Or: "To be honest, your son is batting seventh instead of third because he's hitting only .175, plus he's also committed fourteen errors in the last eight games." And finally: "Your son hasn't pitched in two weeks because he's walked twenty-five batters and only struck out three hitters. On top of that, he's hitting only .175 and committed fourteen errors in the last eight games." In other words, numbers don't lie!

One last parent/coach story. This was during my high school tennis coaching days. I happened to be the head coach at the time.

In high school tennis, a typical team match between two teams, consists of six singles matches and three doubles matches. The six singles players play in order of strength, with each team's number one player playing the other teams' number one player, the number two plays the oppositions' number two and so on down the line.

In order to determine how a team's players are ranked, the common practice is to play "challenge" matches against teammates. In this way, you work your way up the ladder if you beat your teammate, and down the ladder if you lose. It's a very fair method and there's no questions. You either win or you lose.

This particular season, a father called me during the day and stated he wanted to speak to me that evening. He wanted to be certain the team had finished practice in order that he might speak to me alone. I was certain I knew why. This prominent business professionals' son was playing number four on the team and dad couldn't understand it. After all, the kid had been taking lessons from two different tennis pros throughout the year and was playing weekend tournaments on top of that.

From my observations, having two different coaches (three, if you count me) was his son's biggest problem. He played confused, always switching back and forth between playing philosophies. He also seemed to be exhausted all the time. In fact, he was so confused and tired, he couldn't beat several of his own teammates who lacked the raw talent this kid possessed. He had lost three "challenge matches" in the past couple of weeks. This placed him on the singles ladder at number four. I had written proof, showed the parent the results and, in my mind, the case was closed! The father may have not been happy, but he had no argument against me.

That team, by-the-way, was second at the conference championship that year. This was the highest finish ever in the school's history at the time.

The above mentioned player was runner-up in singles for the conference championship at number four singles. He and his partner actually won the championship at the number two doubles position. He was right where he belonged in our line-up. Sorry Dad.

CHAPTER 23 *Coaches' Capers*

The best high school coaches are well respected by their players, parents, administrators and fellow coaches. Some take on a sort of legendary status, but the very finest nearly always are first class role models.

Even the best of the best have "moments in time" where things don't necessarily go as planned. These men among men (or women among women) do certain things that can make us question even their sanity. Things happen or they make choices that remind us they are just people, too. Great coaches, but just people.

Following are some odd or unique experiences involving coaches that I know. I know they took place because I was there when they happened.

Years ago I was assisting a high school sophomore baseball team. For several years prior to that, I had been the school's varsity assistant baseball coach, and had also spent one season as the head sophomore coach. We had a very successful program for many years with not one losing season seventeen years running.

This year, the school had hired a new coach to run the sophomore program. I had been asked to "move down" for a year to use my "years of experience" to quietly help the new coach. It was to be for only a year until he was more established, and felt comfortable coaching fourteen to sixteen year old high school boys. His experience coaching baseball up until he took the position had been mostly at the Little League level. This was a definite step up and going to present many new challenges for him.

Coaching at any level is difficult enough for a veteran youth coach, let alone someone brand new to the high school level. Parents, scheduling transportation, practice lesson plans, scheduling practices, media relations and, of course, parents can make life in high school baseball seem more like work at times. It can take away small parts of the enjoyable game baseball was designed to be.

I remember quite well working with the new coach, who was a touch rough around the edges early on, but confident and very capable with his new assignment. We got along great, meshed our philosophies well and seemed to complement each other. We were enjoying a very successful season.

We were about half way through the season. The team was playing on a warm, sunny Saturday in a four-team tournament that our school was sponsoring. We were in the first base dugout as we traditionally had been for years.

Our team was well ahead score-wise, to a much less talented opponent. We had one of our best pitcher's on the mound. Throwing with above average speed was his forte. Throwing strikes was not. Because of this, many of the opposing batters were swinging late, unable to consistently catch up with our pitcher's fastball.

Our head coach was standing in the entrance to the dugout, with the rest of the team, including myself, located inside.

The batter from the opposing team, a right handed hitter, was just stepping into the batter's box. On the first pitch, he hit a ball directly over the top of our dugout, a sure sign that he was swinging quite late at the ball. He was definitely over-matched by our hurler.

Immediately after the foul ball, the head coach, still standing in the dugout's entrance, warned our players to "be alert" due to the lateness of the batter's swing. The ball could be heading our way with very little warning and tremendous velocity.

On the very next pitch the batter swung and once again, swung very late. With a mighty cut, he hit a screaming line drive that came rocketing directly at our dugout. He hit it like an arrow towards the entrance of our dugout, where our head coach stood like an enormous bullseye.

The ball headed at the dugout like it was being directed by precision radar. It was hit right at the unprotected coach. The coach quickly ducked and turned his head to one side. It was a valiant effort, but to no avail. The baseball sped by the coach, grazing the side of his head and making nearly full contact with one of his ears. It struck the ear with enough force to actually "rip" a portion of the bottom part of it. Although he completed the game as a "walking wounded", it appeared to me stitches would be a necessity after the conclusion of the game. I don't recall if that were the case, but I do remember a sizable bandage on his ear a couple of days later. It was a classic case of

"Do what I say, not as I didn't do what I said you should do".

Athletic coaches are very busy guys and gals. They have much to deal with and much to be concerned about. An enormous amount of headaches come with the job for the minimal amount of pay they receive. It's easy for the mind to be thinking of numerous things at one time, when you should be thinking of what's taking place in the present, what just happened in the past and what you know might be coming in the near future.

It was one of those evenings for an excellent coach I once assisted. It was the second game of a double-header and the heat and humidity were nearly off the charts. We were in the hunt for a league championship, but our hitters were struggling that night and we were in need of a pitching change.

Our team had just been set down in order, putting our squad back in the field on defense. Our head coach hustled from his position in the third base coaching box to the dugout, stopping our team to huddle them together, prior to re-taking the field. After alternating, first, a few encouraging words, and then, several choice words about their level of play, the coach, whose mind was spinning wildly, took off on the dead run back to the third base coaching box. There, he took his customary position. He was ready for something good to happen. Problem was, of course, the opposing team was now up to bat. The coach looked in to see a player wearing the wrong color of uniform about to take his place in the batter's box! The opposing coach, who was standing close by, had been chuckling for some time.

In hopes of being inconspicuous, the coach made his way out a gate close to the third base dugout and circled behind the bleachers. He jogged his way "behind the scenes" all the way back to our dugout on the first base side. Total embarrassment was partially avoided.

One final "coaching story" to show others that when it comes to "the boys of summer", coaches are sometimes the biggest kids of all:

Speed in baseball is fascinating. Speed comes in many forms including running speed, bat speed and the speed it takes to make a decision on defense. The most discussed form of speed in the game is that of the throwing velocity of pitchers. In the major leagues, the average speed of pitcher's fastballs is well over ninety miles per hour. One Major League pitcher has recently been clocked at more than one-hundred and five miles per hour!

One night during a high school practice, we had our players finish up by taking batting practice off the teams' pitching machine. We used a radar gun to set the machine at approximately eighty miles per hour, which is the speed of a decent high school pitcher.

After the team finished practice and everyone had left the field, the head coach and I realized that in all the years we had coached together, we had never jacked the pitching machine up to full bore to see what its' capabilities were. We decided this would be the night. As the head coach cranked the machine up as high as it could go, I put on a batting helmet and armed with a bat, headed to the batters' box to begin the process of taking my life into my own hands.

We were ready. The coach had the radar gun in one hand as he dropped the first ball into the machine. POOF! The ball headed towards home plate faster than I had anticipated. I had faced ninety mile an hour fastballs in college, but this was unreal. I think I may have seen the pitch; I do know that I heard it as it whistled by me. I wasn't prepared for what I saw (or heard) and didn't swing. I thought to myself, if the balls' trajectory gets off course for any reason, this could be my last day on earth! Best case scenario I would be severely injured with some part of my body in pain or deformed for the rest of my life! "Holy cow! One-hundred and three miles per hour!" the coach yelled in excitement.

The next six or seven pitches were all at one-hundred three or one-hundred four miles per hour! I didn't touch one. Then finally, on about the eight pitch, I fouled one off. Success! Soon after I hit a ground ball and finally lined a ball to right field.

Unless a person experiences the velocity of a one-hundred plus mile-per-hour fastball first hand, they could never appreciate it. I admit I was in my late forties at the time, so I didn't have the bat speed I possessed twenty-five years earlier. Even so, it would have been unbelievably difficult even at age twenty three. Ted Williams once said that the hardest thing in all of sports, is to hit a fastball; to hit a round ball with a round bat. Trust me. I'm a believer.

CHAPTER 24 *Kids Do the Weirdest Things*

Coaching youth can be one of life's ultimate positive experiences. That is if you put in the time and effort to "do it right". Unfortunately, "right" can have many definitions depending on who you talk to. For as many youth sport coaches that are in the world today, there's a high probability that you will find as many definitions as to what is the "right way" to be a successful coach on the field or on the court. There are many styles out there.

My own personal definition or philosophy in a nutshell comes down to a leader who can begin by teaching a child or young adult the proper fundamentals of the game. This person must be able motivate and instill enthusiasm into his/her charges. The coach is someone who through it all must be able to communicate to his or her players that the game is just that, a game. It's not a life or death situation. Kids should look forward to not only playing in actual game situations, but should enjoy coming to practices, too.

I believe in teaching respect by showing respect to every player, fellow coach, administrator and parent regardless of the skill level or the personality of the athlete. Above all, I want the young athletes to learn characteristics and traits that they will be able to use throughout their lifetimes. Discipline, dedication, team work and a good work ethic to name an important few.

Sounds like pretty serious stuff, doesn't it? Done well, it is and should be. But being a part of a boy or girls' life that can help mold them into men and women with strong moral views and high ethical standards, should be taken seriously. To do all this and still keep the fun and excitement in the overall experience is not easy and takes a great deal of long, hard work.

With that said, all the seriousness involved in coaching youth cannot stop the fact that at certain times, kids are going to be kids. They will forever be doing strange or unusual things no matter what.

Many unusual stories took place while I was working very hard to put true meaning into young lives. Here are three of those stories. They come from three different levels of teams I coached over the years:

In a previous chapter I discussed tee-ball and a rundown on statistics associated with coaching four to six year olds. I'll start at that level.

Our team (I use the word "team" loosely in this case) was in the middle of a hotly contested match of two remarkably evenly matched opponents. Both teams may have had one "player" who could actually hit, field and throw a ball with some tiny resemblance to a baseball player.

Our group of very short people was playing defense at the time. A little boy on the other team was standing at the tee. He took a healthy cut and surprisingly made good contact with the ball, sending a hard ground ball that as usual went by or under several of our defenders. It ended up well out in left field.

When the ball finally stopped rolling and came to a halt, I came to the realization that our left fielder wasn't there! Where was he? Oh please, I hope he hadn't been kidnapped! I looked all over the field. No, he wasn't on the diamond anywhere! I checked the bench area thinking he might have decided to get a drink of water, or maybe he just decided to head to the sideline to talk to Mom or Grandma. Wrong again.

About that time, I heard several parents yelling and pointing towards a playground located about one-hundred and twenty-five feet past the normal left field position. I looked in the direction of the playground and there, just jumping off a swing, on and on his way to the "monkey bars", was our AWOL left fielder. Apparently becoming bored with the game, he decided to hit the playground to burn off a little energy.

Needless to say, the move cost us a run (not that anyone really cared) as the ball lay motionless in left field and the little slugger circled the bases without worry.

I wonder if Lou Brock ever abandoned his position in left field to go play cards or maybe hit the concession stand for a hotdog?

The next story happened when I was helping coach a minor Little League team. These are the eight or nine year old players I spoke of earlier. This age-group is just getting their first taste of real baseball. They get to wear real uniforms, face live pitchers their own age, and the score is kept. Now, there's a winner and there's a loser. It's literally a whole new ball game! It's a form of real baseball!

It was the first game of the season. Everyone was excited, especially the eight year old "rookies". A warm April day, fresh cut grass, chalked foul lines and batter's boxes, plus the great smells coming from the concession stand. It couldn't get any better for young boys dreaming of playing in the big leagues someday.

Our team was warming up taking infield/outfield practice prior to the start of our game. I noticed our second baseman was struggling in some odd way. It was apparent he was having difficulty moving. He couldn't run, throw or bend over without grimacing. I assumed he must have had some type of accident recently.

He struggled mightily through our pre-game drills from start to finish. As the team ran off the field and headed towards our dugout, I could see our poor little second baseman was limping badly. As he entered the dugout, I stopped him in hopes of diagnosing his problem. As much pain as he seemed to be experiencing, I thought I might need to speak to his parents and find a replacement for him for the fast approaching game.

Without going into a lot of detail, after a series of questions directed at our little second-sacker, I thought just maybe, I had it all figured out. Not only was this his first time for wearing a real baseball uniform, but also the first time for wearing the protective gear that goes under the uniform. Yes, this was his first experience at wearing a protective cup. For those unfamiliar with a "baseball cup", it's a somewhat triangular plastic gem that was designed to protect a baseball players' "gems". The cup was a fantastic invention that has saved many a baseball player (of all ages) from speaking an octave or two higher than God had intended them to.

After a series of basic questions, I asked the little guy if the cup might possibly be the issue that had the potential to land him on the "disabled list", if it wasn't corrected? He agreed that this might very well be the case. He then proceeded to unbuckle his belt, unzip his baseball pants and reach in and pull out the little piece of plastic armor.

Once he did, it was apparent what had been causing him major discomfort. He had been wearing the cup upside down! Once I explained to him the proper method to position the cup, he went on that evening to play the game with the youthful enthusiasm and vigor that was expected of an eight year old boy. Most importantly, he played pain free!

Cell phones were just coming into vogue with the younger set on this final story. Not many kids possessed one at the time, but those who did were already quite adept at abusing their use.

I was helping to coach a Senior Little League team, boys ages thirteen and fourteen. It was a talented team in relationship to the rest of the league. While the team ended up being league champions, they were quite a lively bunch and didn't always have baseball on their mind. This is pretty much standard procedure for nearly all boys in this age group.

It was the late innings of a "blow-out" game. Our team was winning by a wide margin, in what quite honestly had turned into a boring "snoozer" of a contest.

Admittedly, things had gotten a little lax in the dugout and it took a consistent effort by the other coach and myself to keep the team engaged in both the dugout and on the field.

I was looking forward to the completion of the game, when I happened to glance out at our right fielder. To be honest, our right fielder was unquestionably, the worst player on our team and had to rank in the top three worst players in the league. He was playing for one of two reasons: either because his best friend was on the team or because his parents were forcing him to do so. It may have been a little combination of both. Whatever the case, he had no desire to play baseball.

When I looked out into right field, I could see baseball was no concern of his at the time. He was talking on his cell phone! He was in the middle of a major conversation as our pitcher delivered the ball. In all my years of coaching, I've seen nearly everything. This little episode put "everything" just that much closer to being reality.

After a semi-brutal vocal beating coming from the coaching staff in the dugout; the cell phone found its' way to the right fielder's back pocket. A final definitive tongue lashing once the player reached the dugout, put closure on the situation.

Oh, his excuse for talking on the cell phone in the first place? He had "received a call from a Major League scout and was negotiating his new contract." Good try, but when you're hitting below .150 and your fielding average is nearly identical to your batting average, I'm pretty sure that wasn't the case.

CHAPTER 25   *The Never Concluding Conclusion*

Sports, it's an American passion. A high percentage of males and females from ages three to one-hundred play, coach or are spectators.

Americans love to watch all ages and skill levels from the youngest who virtually have no skill to the grossly overpaid professionals who possess the highest skill level of all.

We all enjoy watching the routine plays, the great plays, and even like to see the mistakes.

We giggle at the mistakes youngsters make, as they're expected to make them. We tend to get upset when our favorite professionals make mistakes. After all, they're paid handsomely not to make them.

However, I do think, we sometimes get a little bit of satisfaction seeing a fabulously wealthy "pro" make a miscue. Seeing this, gives us a small sense that these players are not super human, but just people like us. After all, any of us could drop a ball or strike out and we wouldn't have to be paid ten million dollars annually to do it. Shoot, we'd be happy to take a salary cut from the team and play for say, a measly two-million dollars a year. The team could get the same results and save eight-million dollars per year!

Of course that's not going to happen, so most of us are relegated to watching the rich and famous athletes. We see the game unfold in front of our eyes, and enjoy the game for what its' worth.

But, as the previous stories have indicated, there's a great deal of behind the scenes "goings on" that truly complete sports and help to make the games we love that much more special.

I'll leave you with some other behind the scenes "happenings" that I've been involved with, without going into a lot of detail. While none of these contributed directly to the final score in an obvious way, some may have had an indirect relationship in some form or another. These antics come from a variety of sports. They include:

- Squirt gun fights (in a baseball dugout).
- Sun flower seed spitting contests for distance (again, in a baseball dugout).
- Eating of a birthday cake on the bench (cake hidden on a basketball bench).
- Sports trivia contests among players with the coach giving out the questions (in a baseball dugout with prizes included).
- Music trivia contests: "Name that Tune" or "Name that Band" from songs being played on a public address system or in cars or busses on road trips (baseball and basketball).
- Assigning "nick names" to each and every player and coach on the team. Usually the coach never finds out his nickname (in a baseball dugout).

- Making up new riddles that could go on "Laffy Taffy" wrappers (in the baseball dugout). Example: "How did the chicken get from first base to home plate? Answer: "Balk, Balk, Balk"! (Think about it)
- The telling of some really good and some really bad jokes (all teams and running groups).
- The placing of a unique good luck charm that each baseball player touches when he enters or exits the dugout. (coins, miniature trolls, G.I. Joe dolls, among others)
- Touching third base when running off the field to the third base dugout and stepping on first base when running to the first base dugout. A common baseball superstition.
- Timed juggling contests with three baseballs or tennis balls. No prizes to the winner, just the satisfaction of being the best for the day or holding the "season record".
- Taking turns retrieving foul balls, as bench warmers, and timing each other to see who can set the all-time season record for getting back to the dugout the fastest. Also, to see who can retrieve the most balls during a game.
- The moving and hiding of a teammate's Volkswagen Beetle by half a baseball team and their friends before the player returns to the parking lot after an away baseball game.
- Just like a scene in the movie "*A League of Their Own*", a shortstop intentionally letting loose with an errant throw in the general direction of a boisterous fan to keep him quiet. It worked!

Yes, weird and funny things go on all the time when it comes to sports. Next time you attend an athletic event of any kind, keep this in mind. With a little luck and an increased awareness, you might just see or hear something you've never experienced before or ever will again!

About the Author

Lyle was born and continues to live in Burlington, Iowa. He and his wife Janice have been married for forty-three years. They have three grown sons, Jason, Justin, and Jonn.

He is the author of the best-selling book *"A Lifetime in Motion: Lessons Learned from a Student of the Game(s)"*.

He graduated Summa Cum Laude with a Bachelor's Degree from Monmouth (Illinois) College and holds an MBA from California Coast University.

His former high school baseball coach, Dick Wagner, who was National High Baseball Coach of the Year in 1972 and Iowa High School Baseball Coach of the Year in 1971 and was also Athletic Director at Burlington (Iowa) High School for many years; once stated that Lyle was the "purest" right handed hitter he ever coached in baseball. He has introduced Lyle as the "best all-around athlete ever to come out of Southeast Iowa.

- He was a two-time All-State second baseman at Burlington High School.
- As an adult, he's participated on five National Championship baseball teams in the National 50/60 and Over Baseball Tournament.
- Lyle has coached high school baseball, mostly as an assistant, for 21 years, winning 454 games and losing 222 in that time frame.
- He was a member of the United States Professional Tennis Registry for many years, making his living in the tennis business.
- Lyle has run 16 marathons, having qualified for the Boston Marathon seven times, and ran the Boston Marathon on two occasions. Prior to coaching

baseball, Lyle coached high school tennis for 10 years. During his tenure, he won Burlington High School's first Conference Championship in school history and was named Conference Coach of the Year.
- He has also served as a volunteer in the community in a wide array of events over the years.
- He has been Race Director, Co-Race Director or Course Director for numerous road races in the Southeast Iowa Area.
- He is a widely sought after speaker for Parkinson's Advocacy.

Made in the USA
Lexington, KY
27 April 2018